How To Start A Business With ChatGPT

Jon Adams

CONTENTS

INTRODUCTION

In the swiftly evolving landscape of entrepreneurship, "How To Start A Business With ChatGPT" emerges as a vital handbook for the modern business founder. At the heart of this book lies a singular promise: to elucidate the dynamics of harnessing the power of ChatGPT, an advanced AI language model, as a formidable ally in the realm of business creation and growth.

From the first spark of an idea to the complex intricacies of day-to-day operations, this book serves as a navigator, guiding the reader through the thrilling process of business development with ChatGPT as a trusty sidekick. Readers will uncover how ChatGPT can metamorphose from a virtual assistant into an engine of innovation, a sounding board for strategy, and a scalpel for cutting through market complexities.

Each chapter delves into various facets of business, consistently emphasizing the integration of ChatGPT in strategic planning, marketing, product development, customer service, and beyond. The chapters are crafted with a dual focus in mind: to provide you with a repository of sample prompts exemplifying ChatGPT's utility and to offer a depth of insight into the foundational elements of a thriving business.

The essence of the book is not simply in providing lists of commands for AI interaction but in demonstrating the art of conversation with AI to kindle creativity, solve problems, and glean insights that traditional methods might overlook. Whether you're a seasoned entrepreneur or taking your first step into the business world, "How To Start A Business With ChatGPT" is designed to help you leverage a groundbreaking tool to gain a competitive edge and steer your enterprise toward success.

Embark on this enlightening journey to discover how ChatGPT can amplify your vision, streamline your processes, and catapult your business into a prosperous future.

UNDERSTANDING CHAT GPT AND ITS CAPABILITIES

ChatGPT represents the cutting edge of AI's role in streamlining and enhancing the business landscape. With its ability to process and produce language as if it were a seasoned professional, this technology stands as a pivotal tool in the modern entrepreneurial toolkit. Every interaction and conversation through ChatGPT presents an opportunity for businesses to refine their operations, craft their narratives, and engage with customers on a level that was once unimaginable. By harnessing this power, your enterprise can stay not only relevant but also ahead in a rapidly evolving digital world, where communication and efficiency drive success. Understanding this tool is more than an asset; it is a necessity in harnessing AI's full potential to transform your business strategies and customer experiences.

ChatGPT sprang from the research labs of OpenAI, inspired by the surge to create AI that mirrors human conversation. The underlying technology, a transformer-based neural network, represents a significant leap in machine learning, primarily in processing language data. Unlike its predecessors, ChatGPT isn't bound by rigid, rule-based programming; instead, it learns from examples of actual dialogues, much like a keen apprentice absorbing nuances from real-world interactions. It digests vast amounts of text, learning to predict and replicate patterns in language use with startling accuracy.

At its core, ChatGPT is driven by layers of algorithms working in concert, akin to the interconnected sections of an orchestra, each 'reading' different elements of text to produce coherent and contextually apt responses. The model operates on the principles of input and output—given a prompt, it generates a response, refining its output through a process known as reinforcement learning, where it adjusts its answers based on new information, growing more precise with each interaction.

Imagine a complex library where each book is a fragment of conversation, and ChatGPT is the studious librarian meticulously cataloging and referencing each snippet to inform the next visitor. In a sense, ChatGPT is a reflection of our collective discourse, capable of offering both factual information and creative composition.

However, the technology isn't without constraints; it learns from historical data, meaning it can be misled by inaccuracies within those datasets or struggle with extremely novel concepts. Yet, its integration into business systems and customer service platforms highlights its increasing utility. Far from static, ChatGPT's development is an ongoing narrative in the AI field, with each chapter promising more refined dialogue systems that edge ever closer to the seamless mimicry of human conversation. As it stands, both in function and potential, ChatGPT embodies a significant stride towards sophisticated, human-like AI communication.

The transformer neural network that ChatGPT is built on represents a departure from previous sequence processing methods like recurrent or convolutional networks. In essence, transformers handle ordered data, like the words in a sentence, without the sequential computation that defines earlier models. This efficiency is largely due to the self-attention mechanism.

Self-attention allows each input element to interact with all the others, to determine its contribution in the context of the entire sequence. Think of a roundtable discussion where each participant measures the relevance of all the others' comments to best articulate their own contribution. Position encodings are assigned to input data to retain the sequence order — similar to placing a bookmark on pages to remember the order of reading.

Multi-head attention is a layer that facilitates the model to focus on different parts of the input sequence simultaneously, comparable to having multiple readers to extract different viewpoints from a text. These attention 'heads' work collectively, processing the input in parallel, each with its own focus, which ensures nuance and detail isn't lost in the conversation.

The output of the transformer network is then pieced together to form the final response, akin to assembling a jigsaw puzzle to form a complete picture. However, the response generated isn't the end. User feedback enters the picture, guiding the reinforcement learning process.

In reinforcement learning, the model generates several possible outputs, which are then evaluated based on their performance against certain criteria — like customer feedback in a product review. The model, akin to a product improving through iterations based on user reviews, adjusts its internal parameters during retraining for improved responses in future interactions.

For tokenization, consider it like dividing text into its building blocks, words, or phrases, before interpretation. Through evaluation, the model gauges the likelihood of each 'token' or word, akin to assessing the probability of drawing a particular card from a full deck.

The sequence generation, then, is the model combining these tokens in a fluid, contextually meaningful order, much as an author arranges words to form coherent narratives. Consequently, this entire orchestration of processes enables ChatGPT to participate in human-like discourse, offering both informational and creative exchanges.

In operating ChatGPT, you might input a pseudo prompt such as: "Generate a summary of recent developments in renewable energy." The model tokenizes the prompt, assesses each token's relevance, and crafts a response that synthesizes the current facts, figures, and discussions in the renewable energy domain, presenting you with a summary as if compiled by a subject-matter expert.

Transformer models stand out in the field of machine learning by tackling the challenge of sequence transduction, or mapping input sequences to output sequences, with innovative techniques that differ from traditional machine learning algorithms. Traditional methods, such as recurrent neural networks (RNNs) and convolutional neural networks (CNNs), process sequences step-by-step in a linear progression or through local filters, respectively. Transformers, in contrast, comprehend the entire input sequence collectively, capturing the context of each element in one go.

This global understanding is made possible by self-attention mechanisms, which allow for the consideration of the entire input sequence when generating each element of the output. Imagine trying to solve a jigsaw puzzle by looking at the whole picture on the box rather than just focusing on connecting individual pieces; that's how the transformer model approaches problem-solving, providing a bird's eye view of the textual landscape.

The sophistication of transformers is crucial in natural language processing (NLP) tasks, such as translation, summarization, and question-answering, because language is heavily context-dependent. Words take their meaning from surrounding words, making the global approach of transformers powerful in capturing these nuances. This technology enables AI systems to compose coherent and contextually relevant passages of text, interpret the sentiment in given snippets, and even generate creative pieces that feel startlingly human.

Transformers also feature parallel processing, which contributes to their efficiency—rather than handling one word at a time, they process entire phrases simultaneously, comparable to a skilled reader who grasps full sentences in a single glance. This trait is not only a time-saver but also allows for more dynamic interactions with language, providing a smooth and natural flow to the AI-generated textual output.

Despite their groundbreaking capabilities, transformers are not without limitations. They demand substantial computational resources, and if trained on skewed datasets, they can propagate biases. Continuous improvements and mitigations are part of the evolution of this technology, which remains central to achieving more nuanced and sophisticated interactions between humans and machines in the natural language dominion.

Let's take a deeper look at the self-attention mechanism within transformer models and unravel how it processes language. Each word in a sentence is treated as a distinct element, and to understand its role, the model assigns it an attention weight. These weights are like the intensity of the spotlight on an actor on stage—the stronger the light, the more important the actor is in that scene.

To determine these weights, the model performs calculations that consider how each word relates to every other word in the sentence. It does this by generating three representations for each word: the query, the key, and the value. The query is like a question posed about the word, and the key is like the identifying information that helps match it to other words. When the model compares the query of one word to the keys of all the others, it produces scores that reflect their compatibility. These scores are then converted into probabilities using a softmax function, which are the attention weights.

The attention mechanism uses these probabilities to weigh the value representations, which contain the actual content of each word. It's similar to creating a summary of each word's meaning based on how it interacts with the rest of the sentence. The resulting weighted values are summed up to produce a final embedding for the word, a rich representation that contextually situates the word within the entire sentence.

Positional encodings are added to each word's embedding to give the model information about the order of words. This process is essential because, unlike RNNs that read inputs in order, transformers process all words simultaneously. Think of positional encodings as addresses on envelopes that tell the postal service the sequence in which to deliver them.

Understanding the self-attention mechanism is a crucial step in recognizing why transformers represent a significant advance in NLP. They handle language with an awareness of both meaning and order, without the slow sequential processing that prior models required. This ability not only speeds up the language analysis but also enhances the quality of the machine's understanding and output, making interactions more intuitive and response generation more relevant.

Imagine ChatGPT as a budding novelist, set on writing the next great epic saga. Much like an author who meticulously develops characters and story arcs, ChatGPT is trained using extensive datasets, which are akin to the novel's setting, plot events, and character dialogues. These datasets contain real interactions and linguistic intricacies, allowing ChatGPT to understand the texture and flow of human conversation.

As our novelist assembles narratives from life's vast tapestry – weaving dialogues between diverse characters and crafting convincing plot twists – so too does ChatGPT learn to recognize the nuances of language. It absorbs the ebb and flow of discourse, noting the subtleties that give language its color and vibrancy. The AI's 'story' becomes a harmonious blend of countless interactions, reflecting the richness and diversity of human communication.

Understanding ChatGPT's training process through this lens highlights not just the technical prowess of the AI but underscores the importance of storytelling in learning and communication. In drawing from a well of human experiences, ChatGPT gains the ability to not only respond to queries but to anticipate the underlying emotions and intentions, much like a skilled author who knows their audience. This ability to empathize and engage makes it a valuable companion in any human-digital interaction – offering assistance, generating stories, or even providing companionship through lively conversation.

Here is the detailed breakdown of how ChatGPT, akin to how a seasoned novelist might compile their literary works, constructs its understanding and generates knowledge:

- **Collect and preprocess data:**
  - **Assemble raw text from diverse sources**: This involves gathering written material from books, articles, websites, and other mediums to provide a broad base of knowledge.
  - **Clean the data to remove inaccuracies or unusable content**: Similar to an editor revising a draft, this step ensures the datasets are free of errors, redundancies, or any irrelevant information that might confuse the learning process.
  - **Annotate the data to clarify meanings or contexts**: Annotations act as notes in the margin of a manuscript, offering explanations or clarifications that enrich the AI's understanding of the data it's been fed.

- **Train on datasets:**
  - **Use supervised learning to understand direct mappings between inputs and outputs**: This is where ChatGPT learns from examples that have known outcomes, not unlike a writer learning story structure from classic narratives.
  - **Implement unsupervised learning to glean patterns from unlabelled data**: Here, ChatGPT explores large pools of information without explicit guidance, much as a novelist might glean insights into human nature from observation, without someone pointing out each detail.
  - **Engage in reinforcement learning through feedback loops**: ChatGPT hones its abilities by gauging responses to its output, akin to a writer refining their writing style based on readers' reactions.

- **Construct responses:**
  - **Generate potential outputs**: For every prompt, ChatGPT creates multiple 'drafts' or possible replies, much as an author might write several versions of a scene to see which works best.
  - **Score these outputs for relevance and coherence**: These potential

responses are then evaluated for how well they address the prompt and flow logically, similar to a critique group providing feedback on story drafts.

- **Select the most suitable response for a given prompt**: From the top contenders, the most fitting reply is chosen, in the same way a writer selects the perfect ending after many revisions.

- **Refine response generation over time with continuous learning and feedback**: ChatGPT continually improves, learning from each interaction, just as authors grow more skillful with every story they write.

By understanding each of these stages, the reader gains clear insight into the intricate workings of ChatGPT's training process, evoking the thorough craft of novel writing. Each component plays a crucial role, building upon the last to create an AI capable of engaging conversations and versatile interactions.

ChatGPT is the Swiss Army knife of the digital world—a single tool, neatly compacted into a pocket-sized form, that unfurls into an array of blades and gadgets tailored for a wide variety of tasks. In the realm of business, it's like having an entire office block contained in one software package. Need a creative writer to draft compelling blog posts or ad copy? ChatGPT twists out a quill with an endless inkwell. Looking for a customer service guru to handle queries day and night? It pivots out a headset, ready to engage in polite conversation. What about a meticulous analyst to manage data and streamline operations? ChatGPT pops out a calculator and a planner, organizing and predicting with nimble precision.

Each function is honed for versatility, coming together to support an enterprise as a whole. Like the tool's characteristics to screw, cut, or grip, ChatGPT's linguistic prowess adapts to content creation, interaction, or management tasks. The beauty of this digital multi-tool is not just the breadth of its applications, but also the depth with which it can perform each one— rooted in the understanding that each task complements another within the ecosystem of business needs, forging a synergy that propels companies forward into efficiency and growth.

Here is the detailed breakdown of ChatGPT's business functionalities that come together to provide a robust 'office block' of services:

- **Content Creation:**
  - **Text generation for blog posts, copywriting, and product**

descriptions: ChatGPT crafts written content that rivals that of skilled humans, generating creative and informative text tailored to the needs of a business.

- **Style and tone customization to match brand voice**: It can adjust its writing style to emulate the unique voice of a brand, ensuring that all content aligns seamlessly with a company's image.

- **Incorporation of SEO strategies to enhance visibility**: ChatGPT understands SEO principals and can naturally integrate keywords and meta tags to boost search engine rankings, driving more traffic to a business's online content.

- **Customer Service:**
- **Automated response to customer inquiries**: It provides immediate, accurate, and helpful responses to customer questions, improving the overall experience and freeing up human agents for more complex tasks.

- **Processing and interpreting various languages and dialects**: With its language proficiency, ChatGPT can communicate effectively with customers around the globe, breaking down language barriers.

- **Handling high volumes of queries with consistency and accuracy**: Even during peak times, ChatGPT maintains the same level of reliable service, ensuring that customer inquiries are managed swiftly.

- **Operational Management:**
- **Analyzing data trends to inform business decisions**: It parses through large datasets to identify patterns and trends, offering valuable insights that can guide strategic planning.

- **Forecasting outcomes based on historical data analysis**: By examining past data, ChatGPT can project future scenarios, helping businesses anticipate changes and adapt proactively.

- **Optimizing workflows through pattern recognition and predictive analytics**: ChatGPT finds and implements efficiencies within workflows, optimizing business operations through intelligent automation.

This multifaceted functionality enables ChatGPT to cover numerous areas within a business, providing high-quality services that otherwise would require separate specialized tools or teams. Each aspect leverages ChatGPT's AI capabilities to perform tasks intelligently and cohesively, contributing to a streamlined business operation that is dexterous, knowledgeable, and adaptable. It's not just the diversity of tasks ChatGPT can do but the proficiency with which it executes them that makes it such a valuable asset in the modern business environment.

Envision Elon Musk using ChatGPT to fine-tune SpaceX's customer service. By incorporating the AI's learning algorithms, he could simulate and respond to a spectrum of client inquiries, ranging from technical questions about spacecraft to logistical concerns for satellite launches. This simulated interaction would refine ChatGPT's ability to provide rapid, accurate information, effectively supporting the human support team with increased bandwidth and expertise.

Alternatively, consider Indra Nooyi integrating ChatGPT into PepsiCo's product development. ChatGPT could analyze global consumer data, detect emerging patterns, and suggest innovative flavor profiles or marketing strategies aligned with changing preferences. Here, the AI functions as a dynamic tool for data interpretation, generating actionable insights that can guide the conception of new products or the revitalization of existing ones.

In each case, ChatGPT serves as a sophisticated addition to the decision-making process, offering a depth of analysis and breadth of application that can enrich the strategic arsenal of any business leader. These deployments emphasize the practical integration of AI into business ecosystems, showcasing how such technology could augment human intuition and creativity to drive corporate innovation and enhance consumer engagement.

Let's take a deeper look at how ChatGPT could become an integral part of customer service at SpaceX. Initially, ChatGPT would need to digest extensive documentation on spacecraft design and launch procedures, assimilating knowledge from technical manuals, past mission debriefs, and engineering discussions to build its foundational understanding.

As inquiries come in, ChatGPT would employ natural language processing to decipher the nuances of each question, identifying keywords and phrases associated with spacecraft technology. Then, like a seasoned support agent consulting a meticulous internal knowledge base, it would apply its understanding to construct a response that's both technically accurate and phrased in layman's terms when appropriate, ensuring clarity to diverse audiences.

To align with SpaceX's distinct communication style, ChatGPT's outputs would be trained against a model of the company's previous responses, incorporating the tone and terminology that reflect SpaceX's brand and values. The AI would interface with SpaceX staff via an intuitive dashboard, where team members could prompt the AI, review and refine its responses, and manage the flow of customer interactions.

Regular retraining sessions would be scheduled where ChatGPT reviews recent customer dialogs, particularly those involving newly emerged aerospace concepts or updates in space regulation, to keep its responses current and informed. ChatGPT's learning would be iterative, with each interaction fine-tuned by real-time customer feedback and human oversight, gradually enhancing its precision and helpfulness.

This continuous loop of learning and application ensures not only a high standard of support but also an evolving system that's ever-improving, able to assist with increasingly complex inquiries over time. This adaptation is critical for a company like SpaceX, where cutting-edge innovation is the norm and the customer experience can be as dynamic as the industry itself.

ChatGPT steps into the business sphere as a versatile personal assistant, handling a range of activities that free up human colleagues to concentrate on the tasks that require a personal touch. Picture a hectic office morning; ChatGPT starts by organizing the day's schedule, setting reminders for meetings, and prioritizing emails—much like an executive assistant would—ensuring that nothing important slips through the cracks.

For the marketing team, it's as if they have an extra copywriter on hand; ChatGPT drafts promotional material and brainstorms campaign slogans, providing a creative boost whenever it's needed. When the customer service department faces a surge in inquiries, ChatGPT steps in with the helpfulness of a seasoned support agent, addressing customer concerns and managing follow-ups swiftly and reliably.

In operations, ChatGPT becomes the data analyst who tirelessly pores over numbers, offering insights and identifying trends that inform strategic decisions. It's akin to having a diligent expert by your side, one who doesn't tire and continuously learns, ready to offer up-to-date business advice rooted in the latest data.

Each interaction with ChatGPT is an opportunity to streamline daily tasks, allowing the team to focus on complex projects and client relationships. This AI doesn't just perform tasks—it supports and elevates the human element within business operations, demonstrating that technology and humanity, when working in tandem, can drive success in today's dynamic business environment.

Business owners have at their disposal, through ChatGPT, a suite of tools that operate with the precision of expert craftsmen in fields such as marketing, content creation, and customer service. In the realm of marketing, ChatGPT can generate prompts that enable the crafting of targeted campaign messages—think of it as providing the keywords and style guides that a human marketer would use to infuse brand identity into every communication.

For content creation, ChatGPT offers prompts that work like a brainstorming partner. It suggests titles based on trending topics, creates outlines for informative articles, and provides summaries for complex documents, all while maintaining a consistent tone tailored to the business's audience. This is akin to a savvy editor who helps articulate thoughts into persuasive prose.

When considering customer service, ChatGPT serves as a tireless support agent, fielding prompts that represent common customer queries. It processes these queries by tapping into a vast repository of information, then responds with helpful, informative, and personalized answers, much like a seasoned customer service professional would do after accessing a company's knowledge base.

In guiding a curious business owner through the intricacies of this technology, it's paramount to understand that ChatGPT does not replace human creativity or experience but augments it. It simplifies routine tasks, interprets and generates natural language with finesse, and scales operations to manage larger volumes of work while enabling human employees to focus on strategic and interpersonal aspects where they excel. The technology, ever-evolving, bears potential limitations in understanding sentiments or specialized jargon that can be refined with oversight and regular training updates, ensuring its utility continues to grow in sophistication and relevance.

Here are some ChatGPT prompts that revolve around utilizing AI to improve various aspects of business operations:

[**Creating a Marketing Strategy**] - **Objective**: Formulate a marketing plan for a new product launch.
- **Prompt**: 'Create a comprehensive marketing strategy for our upcoming environmentally friendly home appliances line that targets eco-conscious consumers.'
- **Sample Output**: 'To reach eco-conscious consumers, the marketing strategy will focus on digital platforms known for environmental activism, such as eco-focused blogs and green living forums. The campaign will emphasize the product's energy-saving features, use of recycled materials, and commitment to reducing carbon footprint. Partnerships with influencers in the sustainability sphere will also be leveraged...'
- **Follow Up**: Evaluate the strategy for potential gaps in coverage and consider the incorporation of customer feedback to refine the approach.

[**Developing Brand Voice in Content**] - **Objective**: Generate content that aligns with the company's established brand voice.
- **Prompt**: 'Draft an engaging blog post discussing the benefits of using our Smart Home app, reflecting our brand's friendly and innovative personality.'
- **Sample Output**: 'Welcome to smarter living with the Smart Home app! Our latest update isn't just a step towards more convenient living; it's a giant leap for home management. Imagine controlling your entire home with just a few taps...'
- **Follow Up**: Use the response to inspire a series of blog posts and social media content that further cements the brand's digital presence.

[**Efficient Customer Service Models**] - **Objective**: Explore methods ChatGPT could suggest for improving efficiency in customer service without losing personal touch.
- **Prompt**: 'Design a model for a hybrid customer service system that integrates ChatGPT for efficiency while keeping our service personalized.'
- **Sample Output**: 'Your hybrid customer service model will employ ChatGPT for handling common queries and initial customer interactions. For more complex issues, or when requested by the customer, human support will take over. This ensures quick responses and a personal touch where it counts...'
- **Follow Up**: Implement the model on a trial basis and gather data to

assess customer satisfaction levels, making adjustments as needed.

[**Analyzing Sales Data**] - **Objective**: Break down and understand sales figures for strategic planning.

- **Prompt**: 'Analyze our last six months of sales data and report on any significant trends that should inform our Q3 product focus.'

- **Sample Output**: 'Analyzing the past six months, there's been a 20% increase in sales for environmentally friendly products, signaling a strong market trend. This suggests a growing consumer awareness and preference which may be strategic to focus on in Q3...'

- **Follow Up**: Compare the AI-generated analysis with internal sales assessments and strategize based on the combined insights.

[**Operational Workflow Optimization**] - **Objective**: Determine how ChatGPT can streamline everyday administrative tasks.

- **Prompt**: 'Propose a workflow optimization for reducing the time spent on routine administrative tasks using AI-driven software.'

- **Sample Output**: "To optimize workflow, routine tasks such as scheduling, email sorting, and data entry can be automated using AI. The proposed workflow includes using an AI scheduling tool to manage meetings, an AI email assistant to filter and prioritize messages, and AI for automatic data capture and entry into your CRM...'

- **Follow Up**: Assess the practicality of integrating the suggested automation tools into your systems and monitor performance changes over time.

[**Enhancing Product Development**] - **Objective**: Utilize ChatGPT to contribute to the ideation and creative process in product development.

- **Prompt**: 'Suggest five innovative features for a new line of smart kitchen appliances that could provide us with a competitive edge.'

- **Sample Output**: '1. An AI-powered energy usage tracker to optimize appliance efficiency. 2. Voice-controlled interfaces for hands-free cooking management. 3. Modular design elements for customizable appliance configurations. 4. Integration with health apps to suggest recipes based on dietary needs. 5. Automatic inventory management that syncs with grocery delivery services...'

- **Follow Up**: Review the suggested features and conduct a feasibility analysis to determine which ideas can be realistically implemented and the value they would add.

[**Building Consumer Relations**] - **Objective**: Establish stronger bonds with customers through improved interactions.

- **Prompt**: 'Draft a response to a customer's negative review of our product that addresses their concerns and shows our commitment to customer satisfaction.'

- **Sample Output**: 'Dear [Customer Name], we're truly sorry to hear about your experience with our product. We appreciate your feedback as it helps us to improve. We would like to learn more about the issue and ensure we make things right. Could you please contact us directly at...? Your satisfaction is our top priority.'

- **Follow Up**: Adapt the response framework to other customer service scenarios and ensure personnel are trained to maintain the tone and level of attention provided in the draft.

[**Streamlining Customer Feedback Analysis**] - **Objective**: Leverage ChatGPT to make sense of vast amounts of customer feedback efficiently.

- **Prompt**: 'Analyze customer reviews from the last quarter for the most mentioned features that need improvement.'

- **Sample Output**: 'After reviewing customer feedback from the past quarter, the top three frequently mentioned areas for improvement are: 1. The battery life of the portable blender. 2. The user interface of the smart oven. 3. The durability of the non-stick coating in our cookware set...'

- **Follow Up**: Cross-reference the AI analysis with business goals to prioritize product improvements that align with your strategic direction.

[**Optimizing Sales Approaches**] - **Objective**: Refine sales strategies based on a deep dive into conversational data.

- **Prompt**: 'Identify patterns in our sales calls transcripts that correlate with successful conversions and recommend an optimized sales pitch structure.'

- **Sample Output**: 'Successful sales calls frequently included: a clear value proposition early in the conversation, personalized commentary on the client's specific use case, and a concise summary of product benefits. Recommending structuring future pitches to follow this pattern...'

- **Follow Up**: Train sales teams using the structure provided, measure changes in conversion rates, and refine as necessary.

[**Predictive Analytics for Market Trends**] - **Objective**: Harness the predictive power of ChatGPT to anticipate market changes.

- **Prompt**: 'Based on current tech trends, predict what consumer electronics will be most in-demand over the next holiday season.'

- **Sample Output**: 'Analyzing current trends, it is anticipated that portable health monitoring devices, home automation gadgets, and eco-friendly personal transportation options will see increased demand in the upcoming holiday season...'

- **Follow Up**: Use these predictions to adjust inventory levels and marketing strategies, aligning with the expected shifts in consumer demand.

By executing these prompts, you're unlocking the capability to utilize ChatGPT's advanced AI to sharpen various facets of your business operations, from product development and customer service to market analysis and sales strategy. This exercise fine-tunes your understanding of how AI can tap into existing data to uncover hidden patterns, forecast trends, and enrich customer interactions. The experience is one of harnessing a powerful analytical and creative resource that adapts to and supports your specific business goals. Imagine having an all-around consultant who never tires, providing you with insights and support across multiple departments at any time—you'll be leveraging just that to bolster your business strategy.

Executing these prompts allows you to:
- Understand how AI can contribute to creating cutting-edge products and services.
- Develop an enhanced approach towards customer communication that fosters stronger relationships.
- Refine your sales tactics based on data-driven insights.
- Anticipate market changes and prepare your business to meet future demands effectively.
- Streamline operational efficiencies, freeing up valuable time and resources for strategic decision-making and innovation.

Employing ChatGPT for business strategy is akin to having a consultation with a master chess player who can foresee countless games all at once. Just as a grandmaster examines the chessboard and anticipates future moves, weighing potential outcomes and strategies, ChatGPT processes vast arrays of data to generate business insights and foresights. It sifts through historical trends, current market data, and predictive analytics, supplying businesses with a treasure trove of ideas and possible futures.

Imagine sitting across from a strategist who distills years of knowledge into actionable plans; that's ChatGPT, offering myriad scenarios based on complex data the way a sage might offer wisdom distilled from a lifetime of experience. This AI tool does not merely suggest what the next move in the market might be; it helps craft an overarching vision for the enterprise, much like a master strategist who guides you not just to win the game at hand but to refine your playing technique for all games to come. With ChatGPT, businesses gain a partner in strategizing, one that brings a depth of understanding and breadth of knowledge to the proverbial table, continuously learning and adapting to ensure that every move counts toward achieving long-term success.

Here are some Metaprompts that revolve around enhancing business strategy and operational foresight with AI support:

[**Strategic Forecasting Accelerator**] - **Objective**: To create prompts that guide ChatGPT in generating long-term business strategy forecasts influenced by market trends.

- **ChatGPT MetaPrompt**: 'Develop a series of prompts that would instruct an AI to analyze current market trends and predict their potential impact on our business over the next five years.'

- **Expected Output**: Prompts that MBA students or business analysts would use to engage AI in strategic planning discussions and scenario analysis for their enterprises.

- **Follow Up**: Evaluate the relevance of generated prompts against current business challenges and refine them to meet specific strategic goals.

[**Innovation Idea Generator**] - **Objective**: To devise prompts that leverage ChatGPT's capabilities in ideating and conceptualizing new and innovative products or services.

- **ChatGPT MetaPrompt**: 'Construct prompts that will lead an AI to brainstorm innovative product ideas for different industries, factoring in emerging technologies and consumer behavior insights.'

- **Expected Output**: Prompts that product development teams can use to stimulate AI-powered brainstorm sessions, aimed at uncovering groundbreaking ideas and opportunities.

- **Follow Up**: Review the suggested ideas for viability and alignment with company vision, and initiate detailed feasibility studies for promising concepts.

[**Consumer Connect Enhancer**] - **Objective**: To mold prompts that utilize ChatGPT for forging deeper customer relationships through personalized interactions and services.

- **ChatGPT MetaPrompt**: 'Formulate a set of prompts that will direct an AI to craft customized engagement strategies for various customer segments based on their purchasing history and feedback.'

- **Expected Output**: Prompts tailored to marketing and customer relationship managers to help them build AI-assisted communication plans that feel both personal and scalable.

- **Follow Up**: Implement the best engagement strategies and track customer satisfaction metrics to measure their impact.

[**Operational Efficiency Mapper**] - **Objective**: To generate prompts that help use ChatGPT for identifying bottlenecks and optimizing operations within an organization.

- **ChatGPT MetaPrompt**: 'Enlist prompts that can instruct an AI to analyze our internal operations, identify inefficiencies, and propose process improvements.'

- **Expected Output**: Prompts that operations managers can use to guide an AI-based review of workflows and procedures in search of efficiencies.

- **Follow Up**: Test the AI's recommended operational adjustments in control scenarios and implement the most successful ones across the organization.

[**Cultural Change Agent**] - **Objective**: To use prompts that help ChatGPT assist in fostering a positive organizational culture and nurturing leadership development.

- **ChatGPT MetaPrompt**: 'Create a compilation of prompts that would instruct ChatGPT to devise strategies for supporting cultural change and leadership development within a business.'

- **Expected Output**: Sets of prompts for HR or organizational development professionals focusing on leveraging AI to enhance team dynamics, leadership skills, and culture.

- **Follow Up**: Use these strategies as a basis for developing training programs, team-building exercises, and leadership workshops.

By executing these metaprompts, you will gain:

- **Strategic Insight:** A deeper understanding of how present market forces might shape the future landscape of your business, leading to more informed long-term decision-making.

- **Creative Edge:** The ability to rapidly generate a diverse array of innovative product ideas that could differentiate your offerings in the marketplace.

- **Customer Engagement:** Insights into crafting more personalized and impactful customer engagement strategies that could strengthen relationships and loyalty.

- **Operational Clarity:** A clearer view of internal operations with the potential to uncover and resolve inefficiencies, leading to smoother business processes and cost savings.

- **Cultural Cohesion:** Strategies for nurturing a strong organizational culture and developing leadership qualities that are essential for guiding teams and driving business success.

By leveraging metaprompts, you're essentially equipping yourself with an AI co-strategist capable of turbocharging your brainstorming sessions and strategic reviews. The insights and strategies you gain from this partnership could significantly enhance the agility and competitiveness of your business.

ChatGPT stands as a testament to the potential and versatility of AI in the entrepreneurial realm. Through its advanced linguistic models and vast processing capabilities, it has proven itself to be a significant instrument of innovation and growth. Business leaders now have a tool at their disposal that can assess markets, generate creative ideas, and interface with customers on a scale and with a precision that was previously unattainable. The functions of ChatGPT exemplify AI's ability to extend the reach of businesses, enabling smaller teams to operate with the effectiveness of far larger organizations. It levels the playing field, providing access to quality insights and automations that can drive success in a competitive world. As AI technology continues to mature, its role as a partner in entrepreneurship is not only promising; it is becoming essential for those looking to stay ahead of the curve in an increasingly digital market landscape.

IDEATION AND BUSINESS PLANNING WITH CHAT GPT

ChatGPT emerges as a groundbreaking tool that redefines the essence of business planning. In an era where traditional strategies demand a pivot towards more adaptive, data-informed decision-making, ChatGPT steps in as the expert strategist. It equips entrepreneurs with the ability to refine their ideas and strategize with a level of data analysis and creative thinking reminiscent of a boardroom filled with top consultants.

With ChatGPT, the convoluted threads of market research, trend analysis, and competitor study are woven into a comprehensive tapestry that informs coherent, actionable business strategies. This AI assistant embodies the meticulousness of an experienced strategist, transforming oceans of data into focused insights and clear pathways forward. By highlighting its importance in today's data-driven market, the impact of ChatGPT on business planning is crystallized—it's not just an enhancement to existing processes, but a fundamental shift towards a more nuanced and agile approach.

In essence, ChatGPT acts as a multiplier of human intellect, empowering users to navigate complex business landscapes with confidence. It's a tool that does not obscure but clarifies, bringing high-level strategic planning into sharp relief for those ready to embrace the future of business innovation.

ChatGPT wields an assembly of capabilities that position it as an indispensable asset in strategic business planning. Its core lies in the robust language model developed by OpenAI, which has digested a vast dataset of human language. Consider this model a meticulous librarian who has read and indexed an entire library's content, poised to extract precise information when queried. ChatGPT doesn't just retrieve information; it processes and contextualizes it, akin to a seasoned analyst capable of discerning underlying patterns and trends from raw data.

At the root of this AI tool's effectiveness is its deep learning framework, which allows it to generate human-like text with coherence and relevance.

For a business strategist, this translates to gaining an assistant that can provide market analyses, forecast industry shifts, and suggest actionable strategies with a proficiency that rivals human insight. It cross-references the nuance of language with the logic of statistics, offering decision-makers a multifaceted view of the business landscape.

In practice, ChatGPT aids in shaping business narratives, crafting communication tailored to diverse audiences—from investors to customers—and supplementing the human touch with data-driven precision. It's like having a strategist and a data scientist rolled into one, accessible at the click of a button. Yet, one must be aware of its limitations, such as occasional biases in data or the need for guidance to narrow down broad analyses to specifics. Still, the technology continuously evolves, pushing the boundaries of what AI can achieve in strategic business planning.

Ultimately, ChatGPT stands out as a testament to the fusion of human creativity and algorithmic intelligence, guiding planners not only to ask the right questions but also to anticipate the future of business with an informed, confident stance.

Defining Goals and Objectives:
- ChatGPT Prompt: "Generate a list of key objectives for a startup in the sustainable energy sector focusing on short-term gains and long-term market leadership."
- Role: ChatGPT functions as a digital strategist, suggesting objectives based on current sustainable energy trends and successful business archetypes.
- Consideration: Ensure goals align with ethical standards and long-term viability without exploiting short-term loopholes.

Market Research:
- ChatGPT Prompt: "Analyze the current sustainable energy market, identify the major players, and summarize customer needs and wants."
- Role: The AI delves into databases of market research like a thorough investigator, providing an overview of the landscape, competition, and consumer behavior.
- Consideration: Double-check AI-generated data for biases and inaccuracies possibly inherent in the training data.

Idea Generation and Innovation:
- ChatGPT Prompt: "Suggest innovative product ideas for the sustainable energy sector that fill a market gap and meet a high demand."
- Role: ChatGPT becomes a creative partner, brainstorming ideas that meld technological feasibility with customer insights.
- Consideration: Encourage sustainable and responsible innovation that doesn't compromise ethical standards for novelty.

Planning and Strategy Formulation:
- ChatGPT Prompt: "Create a structured business plan for a renewable energy product that includes marketing, operation, and financial strategy components."
- Role: ChatGPT crafts detailed planning documents, piecing together the insights and creative ideas into a strategic blueprint.
- Consideration: Incorporate risk management into strategies to mitigate potential ethical dilemmas or market shifts.

Implementation Guidance:
- ChatGPT Prompt: "Outline the steps necessary to implement our new sustainable energy product's go-to-market strategy."
- Role: Functions as an implementation guide, breaking down the strategy into actionable steps and timelines.
- Consideration: Strategize to uphold fairness and avoid leveraging competitive practices that may be harmful or deceitful.

Feedback and Iterative Learning:
- ChatGPT Prompt: "Draft a template for collecting customer feedback on our new sustainable energy product and suggest iteration techniques based on feedback."
- Role: ChatGPT suggests ways to actively listen to user feedback and iteratively learn from customer experiences to enhance the product or service.
- Consideration: Develop feedback mechanisms that prioritize privacy and transparency, allowing customers to share their honest opinions without manipulation.

Continuous Improvement:
- ChatGPT Prompt: "Propose a continuous improvement process for our business strategy using AI-driven market analysis and trend monitoring."

- Role: ChatGPT provides a vigilant monitor for shifts and advancements in the sustainable energy field, ensuring the strategy stays agile and responsive.

- Consideration: Emphasize an ethics-first approach in improvement strategies, recognizing the importance of maintaining integrity as business scales.

In each step, ChatGPT serves as an auxiliary force magnifying human intelligence and capability. The AI integrates seamlessly into strategic development, offering data-rich insights and creative ideation while adhering to ethical boundaries and challenging potential biases. The continuous loop of strategy, implementation, feedback, and improvement evidences a dynamic, ever-evolving process, indicative of sustainable and competitive growth.

Imagine walking into a room where the walls are whiteboards, filled with the half-finished thoughts of those who came before you, a marker in your pocket ready to connect the dots. This is what it's like to brainstorm with ChatGPT—a digital room where ideas from a multitude of minds are pooled together, waiting for you to pluck the ones that resonate with your vision. Just as technology has transformed a simple whiteboard into an interactive display capable of capturing and combining input from various sources, ChatGPT collects and compiles a vast array of knowledge, weaving it into a rich tapestry of ideas that become the raw material for your business strategy.

Activating ChatGPT for idea generation is like tapping into a brainstorming session that never sleeps. The AI is a silent partner, ceaselessly offering suggestions, questions, and provocations—the kind you might expect from a round table of diverse thinkers, but amplified by the depth and breadth of its encoded understanding of the world. And yet, despite this powerful cognitive swirl, the AI also knows the art of restraint, filtering and refining its offerings to match your query's specifics.

The power of ChatGPT lies not just in the volume of ideas it can generate, but in the way it adapts to your thought patterns, learning as it goes to serve up suggestions that are more in tune with your aims. It's a partner who listens intently, speaks thoughtfully, and, though it may occasionally miss the mark, always strives to elevate the conversation. Through engaging with ChatGPT, you're equipped to navigate the complexities of business ideation with a newfound clarity, all within the casual comfort of a conversation over a coffee—yet with the depth and nuance of a seasoned expert by your side.

Here are some Metaprompts that revolve around the seamless brainstorming experience with ChatGPT for business strategy development:

[**Title**: "Idea Expansion Catalyst"]
- **Objective**: To generate prompts that will help expand on seminal ideas for business strategies.
- **ChatGPT MetaPrompt**: "Generate a series of prompts that solicit comprehensive expansion on emerging business ideas based on current market gaps."
- **Expected Output**: A collection of prompts aimed at deepening the exploration of select business concepts, encouraging specificity and detail.
- **Follow Up**: Examine the expanded ideas for feasibility and potential impact before integrating them into a business plan.

[**Title**: "Diverse Perspective Integration"]
- **Objective**: To create prompts that bring in diverse viewpoints and interdisciplinary approaches to business problem-solving.
- **ChatGPT MetaPrompt**: "Design prompts that encourage exploring a business challenge from the perspectives of different disciplines like economics, sociology, and technology."
- **Expected Output**: A range of prompts inviting multifaceted analysis and solution-building from various academic and professional standpoints.
- **Follow Up**: Merge the insights from these varied angles to form a well-rounded approach to the business issue at hand.

[**Title**: "Market Trend Analyzer"]
- **Objective**: To curate prompts that aid in analyzing and synthetizing market trends for strategic advantage.
- **ChatGPT MetaPrompt**: "Draft a prompt set that instructs ChatGPT to dissect current market trends and predict their evolution for strategic alignment."
- **Expected Output**: Specific prompts leading to detailed analyses of market dynamics and projections of their future trajectories.
- **Follow Up**: Use the trend insights to adjust or reinforce strategic decisions, tailoring your business approach to anticipated market movements.

[**Title**: "Customer Feedback Loop Creator"]
- **Objective**: To construct prompts that turn customer feedback into actionable insights for business growth and product development.
- **ChatGPT MetaPrompt**: "Compose a sequence of prompts that utilize customer feedback to identify strengths, weaknesses, and opportunities for business improvement."
- **Expected Output**: Prompts that engage ChatGPT in providing constructive critiques and suggestions based on customer responses.
- **Follow Up**: Act upon the synthesized feedback to tweak products or services and formulate development strategies.

[**Title**: "Business Plan Sculptor"]
- **Objective**: To shape prompts that enable ChatGPT to assist in sculpting detailed business plans from broad concepts.
- **ChatGPT MetaPrompt**: "Construct prompts that lead ChatGPT to transform rough business concepts into defined, strategic plans with clear goals, actions, and metrics."
- **Expected Output**: A list of prompts that guide the AI in outlining comprehensive business strategies, complete with operational, financial, and marketing plans.
- **Follow Up**: Fine-tune the resulting business plans and prepare them for presentation to stakeholders or investors.
By executing these metaprompts, you will gain:

- **Enhanced Creativity**: Tools to stretch your traditional thinking, leading to innovative and novel business solutions.

- **Strategic Diversity**: Knowledge on incorporating varied perspectives, enriching your strategy with insights from different fields and backgrounds.

- **Market Insight**: A clear understanding of market trends, allowing you to craft strategies that are proactive rather than reactive.

- **Customer Insight**: A direct line to customer feedback, helping you to understand their needs and improve your offerings accordingly.

- **Business Clarity**: The ability to turn broad, ambitious ideas into concrete, actionable business plans with well-defined steps.

Executing these metaprompts translates to elevating one's strategic business approach by leveraging the analytical power of AI, effectively combining human ingenuity with data-driven support. It means honing the capacity to think deeply about every aspect of a business, from ideation to customer interaction to planning for future growth. Each prompt is a stepping stone to more nuanced thinking and a fuller understanding of the complexities that govern successful enterprises. With these prompts, you position yourself not just to map out a potential business path but to pave the road to a realized vision.

The development of a business plan with ChatGPT's guidance unfolds in a series of deliberate and logical steps, each building upon the last. First, identify the foundational goal or mission statement—like choosing a destination before mapping out a route. ChatGPT then acts as a navigator, drawing from a database with the scale and depth of an ocean to chart possible paths.

Next, engage ChatGPT in a deep dive into market analysis. Here, the AI dissects the layers of market data, competitor benchmarks, and consumer behavior patterns as meticulously as a watchmaker examining the gears of a timepiece. This results in a detailed overview, much like a satellite image of the business landscape, upon which strategic planning is based.

With the market context established, craft the core structure of the business plan by prompting ChatGPT to outline sections like the executive summary, marketing strategy, and financial projections. Think of it as drafting the architectural blueprints for a house—each section must underpin the others to ensure the structure's integrity.

As you fill in each section of the plan, ChatGPT serves as both scribe and advisor, suggesting content that aligns with your company's objectives, values, and positioning. In crafting financial plans, for instance, ChatGPT transforms into an analytical accountant, helping you project revenues and expenses in detail.

Throughout this process, refine your plan by continuously iterating with ChatGPT's assistance. It's comparable to sculpting clay on a potter's wheel, where both the artist's vision and the responsive feel of the material guide the creation's final shape. ChatGPT is pliable yet consistent, offering repeated test runs of sections or even the entire plan for scrutiny and polishing.

In the final stages, use ChatGPT for reviewing and perfecting the language of your plan, ensuring that it is not only strong in substance but also compelling in its presentation. The completed plan stands as a comprehensive document—the product of a synergistic collaboration between human ambition and the interpretive power of AI. Through this process, a nuanced understanding of both the potential and limitations of ChatGPT unfolds, leading to a business plan crafted with the precision and informed confidence necessary for success in the competitive business arena.

Here is the breakdown of the specific steps and details for creating the financial projections section of a business plan with ChatGPT's assistance:

- **Start with Revenue Projections**:
  - **ChatGPT Prompt**: "Estimate the annual revenue for a startup in the sustainable energy sector with a customer base projection."
  - **Financial Metrics**: Gross sales, pricing models, and sales frequency.
  - **Data Sources**: Market analysis reports, pricing strategies from competitors, historical data from similar startups.
  - **Ethical Considerations**: Ensure pricing strategy is fair and reflect the true value offered to customers; avoid price gouging.

- **Detail Cost Structure**:
  - **ChatGPT Prompt**: "Itemize the direct and indirect costs for running a sustainable energy business for the next five years."
  - **Financial Metrics**: Fixed costs (e.g., rent, salaries), variable costs (e.g., materials, shipping), and capital expenditures (e.g., equipment, technology).
  - **Data Sources**: Quotes and estimates from suppliers, industry standards, financial statements of similar businesses.
  - **Ethical Considerations**: Choose suppliers and business practices that align with sustainable and ethical standards; consider the impact of cost decisions on stakeholders.

- **Outline Profitability**:
  - **ChatGPT Prompt**: "Calculate expected net profit and profit margin for the first five years in business."
  - **Financial Metrics**: Earnings before interest and tax (EBIT), net

profit, profit margins.
   - **Data Sources**: Revenue projections, cost structure details, industry profit averages.
   - **Ethical Considerations**: Be transparent about profit sources and ensure financial success is not at the expense of environmental or social responsibility.

   - **Predict Cash Flow**:
   - **ChatGPT Prompt**: "Create a monthly cash flow projection for the next two fiscal years based on anticipated earnings and expenditures."
   - **Financial Metrics**: Cash inflows, cash outflows, net cash flow, cash reserves.
   - **Data Sources**: Billing cycles, payment terms with vendors, loan repayment schedules.
   - **Ethical Considerations**: Maintain honesty in reporting cash projections to investors and manage cash reserves responsibly.

   - **Develop Break-Even Analysis**:
   - **ChatGPT Prompt**: "Perform a break-even analysis considering current market pricing and cost estimates."
   - **Financial Metrics**: Break-even point, contribution margin.
   - **Data Sources**: Sales forecasts, variable and fixed cost estimates.
   - **Ethical Considerations**: Account for a fair return on investment for stakeholders while setting realistic sales targets.

   - **Assess Financial Risks**:
   - **ChatGPT Prompt**: "Identify potential financial risks and suggest mitigation strategies."
   - **Financial Metrics**: Risk impact, likelihood, risk-adjusted return on capital.
   - **Data Sources**: Industry risk profiles, economic forecasts, SWOT analysis.
   - **Ethical Considerations**: Prepare for risks in ways that do not compromise the company's values or commitment to stakeholders.

Through this meticulous process, one creates a series of financial statements that predict the future performance of a business. Careful attention to detail is key to producing financial projections that are both realistic and rigorous, which is imperative in business planning to ensure sustainability and ethical integrity. With ChatGPT as a guide, balance the use of AI-generated data with the human expertise that ensures ethical decision-making remains at the core of all financial strategies.

Imagine AI as the architect behind the scenes of pioneering leaps, much like Elon Musk's ventures into space or Sara Blakely's revolution in women's apparel. Musk, launching rockets with SpaceX, oversees the blueprint of progress, where each decision is a calculated step towards Mars. AI could crunch immense data, predicting rocket trajectories and potential pitfalls, much like Musk envisages interstellar travel—guided by science yet fueled by audacious goals. It could have mapped out SpaceX's strategy, evaluating aerospace designs and market opportunities, just as Musk matched ambition with market needs.

Turn to Sara Blakely, who sculpted Spanx from a simple idea into an empire. Picture AI as her strategic partner, sifting through fashion trends and consumer needs with the meticulousness of a master tailor, recommending product designs and identifying untapped markets. It could have woven the fabric of Spanx's business strategy, finding gaps in the industry much like Blakely spotted unfilled niches in women's wardrobes.

In both scenarios, AI acts as the unseen strategist, augmenting human foresight with its computational might. It blends data into decisions, analogous to a chef fusing ingredients into a new recipe, making the complex world of business strategy more digestible. The result? A feast of innovation where data informs daring, and AI-assisted strategies propel businesses to break new ground, mirroring the bold moves of Musk and Blakely.

Let's take a closer look at how AI can be a linchpin in the iterative design processes of aerospace projects like those of SpaceX. At the outset, AI steps in to analyze vast amounts of data ranging from material properties to flight dynamics. This is pivotal in identifying optimal materials and design configurations, much like choosing the right ingredients for a complex recipe to ensure a delicious dish.

In the realm of simulations, AI is the pilot and the test driver, running countless scenario analyses that simulate different flight conditions and stress tests on rocket components. It's akin to forecasting weather patterns for a safe journey, but instead, it predicts the outcomes of various rocket designs under the harsh conditions of space travel. By identifying potential failures before they occur, AI guides engineers to refine designs, ensuring sturdiness and resilience.

During the decision-making processes, AI steps up as the meticulous decision-support system. It processes simulation data, compares it with design goals, and advises on which modifications could bring about the best possible version of the rocket. It's not unlike a financial advisor who crunches numbers to recommend the best investment options, but here the investment is in design choices that ensure the safety and success of space missions.

This AI-driven strategy not only accelerates the design process but it also brings forth a precision in decision-making that identifies the most nuanced design improvements. It's this microscopic attention to detail, scrutinizing every bolt, plate, and circuit, that could lead to breakthroughs in rocket engineering, just as precise attention to detail leads to creating a stunning piece of art.

In this way, AI becomes an indispensable ally in aerospace engineering, turning the complexity of rocket science into a structured, clear, and success-oriented endeavor. It ensures that every step of the design process is informed, calculated, and geared towards achieving the monumental goal of space exploration.

Using ChatGPT to fine-tune and iterate on business strategies is comparable to honing a diamond from its raw form. It begins with the initial assessment, where ChatGPT serves as a keen-eyed assessor looking for both the facets that shine and the flaws that require polishing. Here, a business strategy is broken down into its constituent parts: value proposition, customer segmentation, revenue streams, cost structure, and competitive advantage.

With each iteration, ChatGPT aids in sharpening these components. Take the value proposition, for example—ChatGPT can help refine this statement, ensuring it resonates clearly with the intended audience, much like an editor might refine a thesis statement for precision and impact. For customer segmentation, ChatGPT evaluates the defined segments against available market data, finely tuning the strategy to target the most receptive audience.

Consequently, revenue streams are analyzed for viability, and cost structures are scrutinized for inefficiencies. In this process, ChatGPT acts similarly to a skilled financial analyst, meticulously sorting through forecasts and budgets to maximize profitability and sustainability. Competitive advantages are not overlooked; ChatGPT assesses the unique selling points against competitors' offerings, sharpening them into clear differentiators.

Through the iterative process of refining, testing, and refining again, ChatGPT guides the business strategy towards a state of readiness for the market. This back-and-forth continues until a market-ready plan is as robust as it can be within the aims and resources of the business. Just as a sculptor works clay into a final form after many adjustments, ChatGPT helps to mold the business strategy into a shape best suited to the conditions it will face upon release. The understanding gained from each iteration feeds back into the process, building a strategy that is not only informed by data but is also agile enough to adapt to new information or market shifts.

In essence, ChatGPT streamlines the evolution of a business strategy, reducing the time from conception to market-readiness, all along encouraging an informed, data-driven approach to strategic planning.

Here are some ChatGPT prompts that are designed to assist in various stages of fine-tuning and iterating business strategies for market readiness:

[**Value Proposition Refinement**] - **Objective**: To sharpen the business's core message to resonate effectively with target customers.
- **Prompt**: 'Revise this value proposition to better align with the interests and pain points of our target audience, detailed in the attached customer profiles.'
- **Sample Output**: 'Our product not only meets your everyday needs but also empowers you to make environmentally conscious choices without compromising on quality or convenience.'
- **Follow Up**: Evaluate the updated proposition against customer feedback and adjust accordingly.

[**Market Segmentation Optimization**] - **Objective**: To ensure the business's customer segmentation is accurate and up-to-date.
- **Prompt**: 'Analyze our customer segmentation based on the latest market research and adjust to reflect current consumer behavior trends.'

- **Sample Output**: 'Market research indicates a shift towards mobile-first users, suggesting a realignment of our segmentation to prioritize this demography.'
- **Follow Up**: Apply the refined segmentation to tailor marketing strategies and measure the response rate.

[**Revenue Analysis and Diversification**] - **Objective**: To assess and diversify the business's revenue streams for stability and growth.
- **Prompt**: 'Identify the most stable and profitable revenue streams for our business model and propose new ones based on industry trends.'
- **Sample Output**: 'Recurring subscription models are currently the most stable. Considering industry trends, a tiered subscription could tap into new market segments.'
- **Follow Up**: Implement a pilot for the proposed revenue model and monitor its performance over a set period.

[**Cost Reduction Strategies**] - **Objective**: To decrease expenditures without affecting the quality of products or services.
- **Prompt**: 'Suggest cost reduction strategies for the business that maintain or improve product quality.'
- **Sample Output**: 'By adopting lean inventory methods and renegotiating supplier contracts, costs can be reduced while maintaining product standards.'
- **Follow Up**: Test out the recommended strategies in a controlled environment before full-scale implementation.

[**Competitive Edge Analysis**] - **Objective**: To identify and bolster the unique aspects that give the business a competitive advantage.
- **Prompt**: 'Compare our unique selling points to those of the top three competitors and recommend areas for improvement.'
- **Sample Output**: 'While our product durability is on par with competitors, there is room to enhance customer service for a competitive edge.'
- **Follow Up**: Develop an action plan to enhance the identified areas and set metrics to evaluate improvement.

[**Iteration and Feedback Integration**] - **Objective**: To create a cyclic process for constantly improving the business strategy using customer and market feedback.

- **Prompt**: 'Establish a process for integrating consumer feedback into regular strategy reviews and iterations.'
- **Sample Output**: 'A quarterly strategy review will be set up where customer feedback is the key driver for iterating our business strategy.'
- **Follow Up**: Conduct the first quarterly review and assess the effectiveness of the feedback integration in strategy refinement.

By executing these ChatGPT prompts, you will gain:

- A refined value proposition that speaks directly to the heart of what your target customers really care about, enhancing the appeal of your products or services.
- Updated customer segmentation that reflects the latest market research, ensuring that your marketing efforts are reaching the right audience more effectively.
- Insights into the most stable and potentially profitable new revenue streams, helping to future-proof your business against market volatility.
- Practical, actionable strategies for reducing unnecessary costs, potentially increasing your business's profitability without compromising product quality.
- An understanding of where your business stands compared to competitors, as well as clear guidance on how to sharpen your competitive edge.
- A structured process for integrating customer feedback into your business strategy, which can lead to continual improvement and a stronger market position.

Each prompt is designed to delve into a specific aspect of business planning that is crucial for success. The tailored output can help streamline and focus business efforts where they will be most effective. These prompts provide a framework for strategic thinking that can turn abstract concepts into solid, actionable plans. They can serve as a catalyst for business growth and ensure that strategies are nimble and responsive to an ever-changing business environment.

To harness ChatGPT effectively, consider it as your digital consultant, ready to assist with a wide range of business inquiries. Begin by formulating clear, concise questions or requests, similar to how you would outline a task for a skilled assistant. For example, you might ask, "What are the key features of a successful online marketing campaign for a fitness app?" This specificity enables ChatGPT to provide focused and relevant information.

As responses are received, review them with a critical eye, recognizing that ChatGPT's knowledge is vast but not infallible. If the first set of suggestions isn't quite right, refine your questions, narrowing down the subject or asking for more detailed information on a particular aspect, just as you might when seeking sharper clarity from a human advisor.

Once you've honed in on the insight you need, put these pieces into action. If ChatGPT provided suggestions for customer segments, integrate those findings into your marketing plan by crafting tailored messaging for each group. Should the AI offer a spectrum of potential revenue streams, evaluate these against your business model and consider running small-scale tests to gauge effectiveness.

Throughout this iterative process, keep in mind that engaging with ChatGPT is a dance of give-and-take. The more precise and detailed your input, the richer and more actionable the output will be. Allow yourself the patience to tweak and rephrase as needed, treating the experience as an evolving conversation that guides you toward refined strategies and improved decision-making.

In employing ChatGPT's capabilities, you don't just gain a wealth of data-driven suggestions. You're equipped with the tools to make these insights operational, crafting strategies that stand on a strong foundation of knowledge and adaptability. It's like turning a blueprint into a building, where each iteration moves you closer to the robust structure you aim to create.

Here are some ChatGPT prompts designed to deepen the understanding and practical application of refining business strategies:

[**Assessing Market Position**] - **Objective**: To evaluate the business's current market position relative to competitors.
- **Prompt**: "Analyze the current position of a mid-size software company in the CRM market and compare it with the top three competitors."
- **Sample Output**: "The software company holds 15% market share, ranking third behind Company A (35%) and Company B (25%). Its strengths lie in user experience and customer support, while it trails in market reach and integration capabilities."
- **Follow Up**: Use this information to pinpoint areas of strength to

capitalize on and weaknesses to improve, adjusting the business strategy accordingly.

[**Value Proposition Enhancement**] - **Objective**: To craft a more compelling value proposition for the business's product or service.
- **Prompt**: "Revise our value proposition to highlight the unique benefits of our project management tool, emphasizing ease of use and integration features."
- **Sample Output**: "Our project management tool simplifies your workflow with intuitive design and one-click integrations, enabling seamless collaboration and efficiency."
- **Follow Up**: Test this revised value proposition with focus groups or A/B testing in marketing campaigns to measure its effectiveness.

[**Optimizing Revenue Streams**] - **Objective**: To explore and identify avenues for revenue optimization based on the business model.
- **Prompt**: "Propose strategies to diversify and optimize the revenue streams for an online educational platform."
- **Sample Output**: "Introduce tiered subscription models, certification fees for specialized courses, and corporate training packages to cater to a wider audience and increase revenue."
- **Follow Up**: Examine the feasibility of implementing these strategies and monitor the impact on the business's revenue.

[**Cost-Reduction Tactics**] - **Objective**: To identify potential areas where the business can reduce costs without sacrificing quality.
- **Prompt**: "Suggest practical cost-reduction methods for a manufacturing company without compromising product quality."
- **Sample Output**: "Adopting lean manufacturing principles, renegotiating raw material contracts, and investing in energy-efficient machinery could reduce costs effectively."
- **Follow Up**: Prioritize these methods based on potential cost savings and ease of implementation and start with pilot projects where possible.

[**Iterative Strategy Refinement**] - **Objective**: To establish an iterative process of business strategy refinement involving ChatGPT.
- **Prompt**: "Outline an iterative process for refining a digital marketing strategy using AI and data analytics."
- **Sample Output**: "1. Collect data on campaign performance. 2. Use AI

to analyze customer engagement and conversion metrics. 3. Adjust targeting criteria and content based on analysis. 4. Repeat the cycle after each campaign."

- **Follow Up**: Implement the outlined process with the next marketing campaign, using the learnings to enhance future campaigns.

[**Competitive Advantage Reinforcement**] - **Objective**: To identify and strengthen the business's unique competitive advantages.

- **Prompt**: "Identify three core competitive advantages of our organic skincare brand and suggest strategies to amplify these in the marketplace."

- **Sample Output**: "Primary advantages include natural ingredient sourcing, eco-friendly packaging, and a loyal customer community. Strategies to amplify might involve a sustainability-focused marketing campaign, partnerships with eco-conscious influencers, and community-building events."

- **Follow Up**: Assess the proposed strategies for alignment with brand values and potential ROI, and then implement the most promising tactics.

[**Customer Segmentation Analysis**] - **Objective**: To analyze and refine the segmentation of a business's target customers.

- **Prompt**: "Refine our current customer segmentation for an online subscription service to better tailor our offerings and marketing messages."

- **Sample Output**: "Segmentation should focus on user activity levels, content preferences, and desired features, breaking down into 'Power Users,' 'Casual Users,' and 'Content-Specific Users.'"

- **Follow Up**: Develop differentiated marketing strategies and product development initiatives tailored to each of these refined segments.

[**Market Trend Adaptation**] - **Objective**: To adjust a business strategy to address the latest market trends and customer expectations.

- **Prompt**: "Outline a plan for adapting our fashion retail strategy to leverage emerging trends in sustainable fashion."

- **Sample Output**: "Initiate a 'Sustainable Choice' line, implement a recycling program for used garments, and partner with suppliers who prioritize ethical production methods."

- **Follow Up**: Create a marketing plan to promote these initiatives and monitor sales data and customer feedback for impact assessment.

[**Financial Projections Refinement**] - **Objective**: To detail the process of creating accurate and comprehensive financial projections.

- **Prompt**: "Create a step-by-step guide for developing robust financial

projections for our e-commerce startup."
- **Sample Output**: "1. Estimate monthly sales based on market analysis. 2. Determine fixed and variable costs. 3. Project cash flow, accounting for seasonal fluctuations. 4. Calculate break-even points. 5. Assess profit margin and return on investment."
- **Follow Up**: Apply the guide to generate projections for the next fiscal year, and use this data to inform budgeting and investment decisions.

[**Business Model Iteration**] - **Objective**: To identify and implement improvements to a business's model for increased efficiency and effectiveness.
- **Prompt**: "Evaluate our current business model for a meal delivery service and recommend iterative improvements."
- **Sample Output**: "Improvements could include optimizing delivery routes for efficiency, partnering with local producers to reduce costs, and introducing a subscription-based ordering system for user retention."
- **Follow Up**: Pilot the recommended improvements in selected regions and analyze their effects on service efficiency and customer satisfaction.

By executing these prompts, you will sharpen your business acumen and strategic thinking, treating ChatGPT as a resource for deepening your understanding of dynamic business components and fine-tuning your business approach. Each prompt is designed to delve into an essential facet of business management, whether it's enhancing your value proposition, scrutinizing financial projections, or seizing competitive advantages. As you interact with ChatGPT, you're effectively conducting a comprehensive audit of your business strategy, challenging assumptions and testing new ideas within the simulated experience that ChatGPT provides. This process not only bolsters the robustness of your strategic plan but also equips you with a heightened awareness of business trends, customer needs, and operational optimizations. It's a practice that ultimately steers your entire business ecosystem toward greater efficiency, impact, and innovation.

By executing the provided prompts, here is what will be accomplished:

- Identified and reinforced the unique selling points of a business to outshine competitors.
- Refined the customer segmentation to precisely tailor marketing efforts and service offerings.
- Adapted to the latest market trends, ensuring the business stays relevant and appealing to modern consumers.

- Developed detailed financial projections that inform smarter budgeting and investment strategies.
- Iteratively improved the business model for increased operational efficiency and customer satisfaction.

ChatGPT stands at the forefront of entrepreneurial innovation, offering a dynamic toolkit for brainstorming, planning, and refining business strategies. This chapter has laid bare the transformative potential of AI in streamlining the journey from ideation to market execution. The reader has been armed with a compendium of detailed prompts, each providing a window into ChatGPT's capabilities to dissect and enhance critical aspects of business—from sharpening the value proposition to adapting revenue models in sync with evolving market portals.

The essence of ChatGPT's contribution is its agility in molding vast data into actionable insights, much like a skilled artisan turns raw materials into a finished product. It represents an ally in the entrepreneurial process, equipped to navigate the complexities of modern business ventures. Looking forward, these insights can be wielded to pave pathways in the business landscape, heralding a future where strategic acumen is augmented by the precision and analytical prowess of AI. ChatGPT is not just a tool but a catalyst for change, nudging ideas towards fruition with the meticulous touch of data-driven guidance. It's a harbinger of success for those who harness its strengths, propelling businesses towards goals with clarity and confidence.

MARKET RESEARCH AND ANALYSIS THROUGH CHAT GPT

Market research stands as the backbone of business strategy, offering insights that are crucial for success in any industry. ChatGPT enters this arena with the promise of transforming the vast ocean of data into valuable, navigable streams of information. This advanced AI tool takes on the role of an astute analyst, adept at pinpointing trends, decoding consumer behavior, and providing a clearer view of the competitive landscape. ChatGPT enables businesses to not only keep pace but to stay ahead, offering finely-tuned strategies derived from data analytics that were once buried in complexity. Through its capabilities, nuances of market research are distilled into actionable steps, and what was once the domain of experts is now accessible to all, guiding decisions with the precision of a seasoned market sage.

Market research is a methodical process—one might liken it to a detective carefully piecing together a case. It begins with gathering data, much like collecting witness statements and evidence, to build a comprehensive view of the marketplace. This data spans customer preferences, buying habits, and even the strategies employed by rival businesses. The analysis stage is akin to connecting the dots, where one looks for patterns, correlations, and insights within the information collected. Here, tools and models sift through the data, seeking out the signals amongst the noise.

The interpretation of these findings is, in essence, the detective's conclusion, providing an informed synopsis that can predict customer behaviors, identify market opportunities, and recognize emerging competitive threats. It influences critical decisions, such as entering new markets or adjusting product features, to better meet customer needs. The importance of market research, in its ability to inform and illuminate the path forward, cannot be overstated. It provides a grounding in reality for business strategies that can sometimes be swayed by intuition alone.

Through market research, a business arms itself with a level of understanding about its customers that can drive growth and foster innovation. In a world where market landscapes continually shift like sand dunes in the desert, this practice offers a firm foundation from which a business can stand confidently, adapt, and thrive.

Let's take a deeper look at the detailed mechanisms of data collection in market research. One of the most common methods is a survey, which can vary from short questionnaires to extensive polls. The advantage here is the ability to reach a broad audience quickly, often yielding a large set of data. However, this method might be tainted by response biases, as not everyone in your demographic will take the time to answer, and those who do might not reflect the whole picture accurately.

Another method is the interview, which involves direct communication, typically one-on-one. Interviews can provide deep insights because the researcher can explore subjects in depth and clarify responses immediately. Yet, they too have biases; the interviewer's own perspective can influence how questions are asked and how responses are interpreted, and interviewees might tailor their answers to what they think is expected.

Focus groups gather a small, diverse cross-section of the target market to discuss specific topics. The dynamic interactions can unearth viewpoints one might not see in isolated responses. However, groupthink can occur where the opinion of the most vocal person sways the rest, potentially skewing the results.

Observation is less invasive, not requiring direct interaction with the subjects. It includes watching how customers behave in real-time, often in retail or public spaces. Observation is excellent for unfiltered insights into customer behavior, but it's a time-intensive process and might not provide insights into why customers behave as they do.

Experiments, often conducted to understand cause and effect, can isolate variables and point to clear conclusions. A business might experiment with different pricing strategies to see what yields better sales, for example. Experimental design must be sound, though, as poor design can lead to mistaken causal inferences.

Each method plays a unique role in peeling back the layers of consumer behavior and market trends. Collectively, they form a compendium of instruments that, when used proficiently, give researchers the superpower to predict and plan with confidence. Understanding each method's potential biases helps to mitigate them and blend insights from multiple sources for a more complete and accurate market picture.

Imagine you're in a bustling, aromatic kitchen, and ChatGPT is the master chef at the helm. The kitchen is brimming with ingredients—the raw data of the marketplace. Like a chef selecting only the freshest herbs and spices, ChatGPT sifts through this plethora of information. Using data analysis as its fine sieve, this chef of computation separates the bits that will flavor the dish perfectly from those that might spoil the taste. Just as a chef relies on their sieve to ensure the sauce has the right consistency, ChatGPT filters out irrelevant data, leaving behind only the most relevant insights. These choice morsels are what will inform and season a business strategy, ensuring that when presented to the consumer, the end result is perfectly tailored to their palate—data transformed into an exquisite menu of strategic decisions. This culinary data dance isn't just about blending ingredients; it's about crafting a dining experience tailored to the diner's very taste buds, mirroring how pivotal data analysis is in satisfying the appetite of a business's target market.

Here is the breakdown of specific data analysis techniques used by ChatGPT and their contributions to market insights:

- **Natural Language Processing (NLP)**:
    - **Technique**: Understands and interprets human language in textual data.
    - **Market Insights**: Determines sentiment trends in customer feedback or social media.
    - **Business Strategy Contribution**: Helps shape product development and marketing campaigns to align with consumer sentiment.

- **Predictive Analytics**:
    - **Technique**: Uses historical data and machine learning to forecast future events.
    - **Market Insights**: Predicts future consumer behaviors and purchasing patterns.
    - **Business Strategy Contribution**: Informs inventory management and promotional timing to anticipate demand.

- **Text Analytics**:

- **Technique**: Extracts meaningful patterns and trends from unstructured text data.
- **Market Insights**: Reveals prevalent themes in customer reviews or forums.
- **Business Strategy Contribution**: Guides customer service improvement and product feature enhancements.

- **Classification Analysis**:
- **Technique**: Categorizes data into distinct groups based on similar features.
- **Market Insights**: Segments customers based on demographic or psychographic data.
- **Business Strategy Contribution**: Tailors marketing approaches to specific customer clusters.

- **Regression Analysis**:
- **Technique**: Investigates the relationship between a dependent variable and one or more independent variables.
- **Market Insights**: Measures the impact of pricing changes on sales volume.
- **Business Strategy Contribution**: Assists in setting optimal pricing strategies to maximize profitability.

- **Association Rule Learning**:
- **Technique**: Identifies interesting correlations and frequent patterns, or associations, between dataset items.
- **Market Insights**: Discovers products frequently purchased together.
- **Business Strategy Contribution**: Drives cross-selling strategies and store layouts to increase basket size.

- **Clustering Analysis**:
- **Technique**: Divides the market data into groups that are similar in specific ways.
- **Market Insights**: Identifies distinct market segments without pre-existing labels.
- **Business Strategy Contribution**: Helps create more focused and responsive marketing tactics for each segment.

Each data analysis technique has the power to turn a flood of raw numbers and words into a stream of clear, actionable knowledge. Whether it's understanding your audience better or staying ahead of market trends, these tools equip you to make informed, smart decisions that can propel your business to new heights. Just like having a good map in unknown territory, these data analysis techniques can be your guide through the complex terrain of the business world.

To effectively use ChatGPT for tracking and understanding industry trends, one begins by posing precise questions. For instance, one might ask, "What are the current trending technologies in renewable energy?" ChatGPT processes this by searching for rising patterns in recent articles, reports, and social media discussions. After identifying these trends, the next step is to inquire about their implications, such as, "What impact could solar panel efficiency improvements have on market prices and consumer adoption rates?"

ChatGPT then analyzes the potential outcomes of the trend, using its extensive dataset to forecast possible future scenarios. It might indicate that higher efficiency could lower cost-per-watt and make solar energy more competitive with fossil fuels, leading to increased consumer uptake and market demand. However, ChatGPT's analysis, while insightful, should be complemented with other research methods to account for economic, environmental, and regulatory factors that might influence these projections.

The final stage involves crafting strategies tailored to this insight. Questions like "How should a mid-sized solar company adjust its business strategy in light of these efficiency improvements?" prompt ChatGPT to draw on successful strategies from similar past events, suggest marketing focuses, and recommend investment in R&D or consumer education programs. The nuanced understanding gained here empowers business leaders with a clear, actionable perspective, offering the foresight needed to navigate the market confidently.

Here are some ChatGPT prompts that focus on leveraging AI for market research and strategic analysis:

[**Emerging Tech in Renewable Energy**] - **Objective**: To identify the latest technological advancements in the renewable energy sector.
- **Prompt**: "List the emerging technologies in renewable energy that have

surfaced in the last year."

   - **Sample Output**: "Recent advancements include improvements in solar photovoltaic efficiency, offshore wind turbine designs, and advancements in energy storage technologies such as solid-state batteries."

   - **Follow Up**: Investigate how these technologies could fit into existing business operations or create new opportunities for expansion or investment.

[**Solar Panel Efficiency Impact**] - **Objective**: To analyze how improvements in solar panel efficiency may influence the renewable energy market.

   - **Prompt**: "Evaluate the potential market effects if the next generation of solar panels achieves a 40% efficiency rate."

   - **Sample Output**: "A 40% efficiency rate could significantly lower the cost of solar power, potentially leading to a broader adoption in residential areas and utility-scale solar farms, and disrupting the current energy market prices."

   - **Follow Up**: Consider how to adapt marketing and production plans to prepare for a surge in demand or changes in consumer preferences.

[**Strategic Planning for Solar Businesses**] - **Objective**: To formulate a strategic plan for a mid-sized solar energy company based on industry trends.

   - **Prompt**: "Given the advances in solar technology, propose a five-year strategic plan for a medium-sized enterprise in the solar industry."

   - **Sample Output**: "The strategic plan includes doubling down on R&D to incorporate new efficient solar panel technologies, expanding to emerging markets with high solar potential, and partnering with smart home companies for integrated energy solutions."

   - **Follow Up**: Discuss the strategic plan with key stakeholders and make adjustments based on their feedback and insights.

[**Competitive Analysis of Solar Firms**] - **Objective**: To compare competitive strategies in the solar industry.

   - **Prompt**: "Assess the strengths and weaknesses of the top three solar panel manufacturers' market strategies."

   - **Sample Output**: "Manufacturer A has a strong R&D focus but lacks marketing presence; Manufacturer B has extensive market reach but is not innovating quickly; Manufacturer C has balanced marketing and innovation but struggles with distribution efficiency."

   - **Follow Up**: Use this analysis to identify strategic gaps and opportunities in your own business strategy.

[Long-Term Effects of Cost Reduction] - **Objective**: To project the potential long-term effects of significant cost reductions in solar panel production.

- **Prompt**: "If the production cost of solar panels were to decrease by half over the next decade, what could be the long-term effects on the solar industry and global energy markets?"

- **Sample Output**: "Such cost reduction could lead to widespread adoption of solar panels, dominance of solar power in the renewable sector, and considerable shifts in global energy politics and economic zones of influence."

- **Follow Up**: Create contingency plans for various scenarios and consider partnerships or investments to take advantage of these shifts.

By executing these ChatGPT prompts, you will gain:

- A comprehensive view of the latest technological advancements that are shaping the renewable energy sector, giving you a fresher perspective on where the industry is headed.

- Insights into how increased solar panel efficiency could disrupt market dynamics, which will help you anticipate changes and plan for future consumer needs.

- Concrete ideas for strategic planning that align with the evolving landscape of the solar energy market, ensuring your business remains competitive and adaptive.

- An understanding of the competitive strategies of leading solar panel manufacturers, providing you opportunities to refine your own company's approach.

- Projections of the long-term effects of cost reductions in solar panel production, allowing you to create strategies today that prepare your business for tomorrow's market transformations.

With these tailored insights, you will be better equipped to make informed decisions that position your business for success amid the ever-changing tides of the industry.

Think of ChatGPT as a keen detective in the bustling city of commerce, one who's tasked with uncovering the secrets of competing businesses. Just as a detective would use various methods to gather clues — from interviewing informants to analyzing records — ChatGPT combs through digital footprints: social media sentiment, online reviews, press releases, and even website changes. These are the tell-tale signs that reveal not only what

49

businesses are planning but also where they might be vulnerable — their unguarded window or weakly-locked door. ChatGPT pieces together these details with the methodical precision of Sherlock Holmes, crafting a comprehensive picture of a business competitor's strategic landscape. It's the shared cups of coffee and whispered rumors of the business world, condensed into tangible insights that show not only how competitors are moving but also why and where they might stumble. Engaging with ChatGPT for competitive intelligence is like having a trusted informant who's always on the beat, ensuring you are well-informed with the latest developments in your industry.

Let's take a deeper look at the intricate process that ChatGPT employs to sift through social media sentiment using natural language processing (NLP). At its core, NLP allows ChatGPT to interpret the vast array of human communication on social media platforms, much like decoding a secret language. Sentiment analysis is a specific NLP technique where ChatGPT examines the words and phrases people use when they talk about a business or product online.

Picture ChatGPT as a linguist, dissecting each sentence to understand the mood it conveys. The AI detects specific keywords—adjectives, adverbs, and even emojis—that are often associated with positive or negative sentiments. It scores these words, weighting them based on their significance in the sentence. This scoring isn't just a simple tally; it's an evaluation of the subtleties of language, where context matters just as much as vocabulary.

Through this detailed linguistic analysis, ChatGPT assembles an emotional profile of what people feel about a competitor's brand. Are there bursts of joy when a new product is launched, or is there a ripple of dissatisfaction about customer service? ChatGPT draws out these emotional undercurrents, surfacing patterns that might indicate a growing delight or brewing discontent.

Understanding the sentiment towards competitors is more than gauging popularity—it's about predicting shifts. Positive buzz could signal a competitor's rising market share, while widespread complaints might foretell a dent in their reputation before it's reflected in sales numbers. Thus, by interpreting the emotions behind customer feedback, ChatGPT provides businesses with early warning signs or opportunities they can act upon, from refining their own messaging to preempting market shifts.

In presenting these insights, ChatGPT equips decision-makers not with raw data, but with a narrative of public perception—a story woven from the very voices of the marketplace. With this knowledge, companies can navigate with foresight, their strategies informed not by guesswork but by the measured pulse of consumer sentiment.

To craft a value proposition using ChatGPT, start by clearly defining the product or service. Consider a specific example, such as a smartphone with a revolutionary new camera feature. Next, interact with ChatGPT by asking it to list the unique features and benefits of the camera. The discussion could involve its ability to capture images in extreme low light, or its advanced image stabilization that allows for professional-level photography.

Following this, inquire about the target market for such a feature. ChatGPT might analyze current market trends and suggest that this camera appeals to travel enthusiasts who enjoy photography or social media influencers who need to produce high-quality content on the go.

Armed with feature lists and target market data, the next step involves refining the language. Ask ChatGPT to translate these features into benefits that resonate with the target market. For the camera, this could mean emphasizing the capacity to capture flawless photos in any conditions, enhancing the user's experience and enabling them to share their world with unparalleled clarity.

Once the benefits are articulated, it's important to position them in relation to competitors'. Request ChatGPT to identify competing smartphone cameras and explain how this new technology outperforms them. It may point out superior sensor technology or proprietary software that competitors lack.

Finally, assemble the value proposition statement by integrating the information gleaned from the previous steps into a concise declaration. ChatGPT should combine the unique features, the expressed benefits to the target market, and the competitive advantages into a compelling narrative. The value proposition for the innovative camera might read: "Experience the world in stunning detail with our smartphone's cutting-edge camera—where leading technology meets professional quality, in your pocket."

This step-by-step process not only yields a clear value proposition but also ensures it's underpinned by real attributes that mirror the consumers' desires and needs. It's like sending a beacon into the marketplace that captures the attention of the right audience and demonstrates unequivocally why your product is the one they've been waiting for.

Here are some ChatGPT prompts that revolve around crafting a compelling value proposition:

[**Feature Breakdown**] - **Objective**: Identify the key features of your product.
- **Prompt**: "List the innovative features of our product and explain the technology behind them."
- **Sample Output**: "The product features include a tri-lens camera system utilizing AI-powered computational photography, a graphene battery for extended life, and a military-grade build for enhanced durability."
- **Follow Up**: Analyze which of these features are most likely to resonate with your target market and consider how they address specific pain points or desires.

[**Target Audience Analysis**] - **Objective**: Determine the target market for your product.
- **Prompt**: "Describe the ideal customer profile for a smartphone built with professional-grade photography in mind."
- **Sample Output**: "The ideal customer is a professional or hobbyist photographer who values high-quality imagery and is often on the go, requiring a durable device with long battery life."
- **Follow Up**: Match the features of your product to the needs and desires outlined in the customer profile to ensure relevance and appeal.

[**Competitive Comparison**] - **Objective**: Position your product against the competition.
- **Prompt**: "How does our product's camera system compare against the leading competitors in terms of image quality and functionality?"
- **Sample Output**: "Our camera system ranks top for image quality in low-light conditions, offers superior zoom capabilities, and features a unique AI that assists in composition and settings adjustments for optimized photo capture."
- **Follow Up**: Use this information to develop marketing messages that

clearly differentiate your product from competitors on key selling points.

[**Translating Features to Benefits**] - **Objective**: Convert product features into consumer benefits.
- **Prompt**: "Convert the technical specifications of our latest smartphone camera into tangible benefits for users."
- **Sample Output**: "The triple-lens setup means you capture every detail, the extended battery life ensures you never miss a moment, and the durable build lets you adventure worry-free."
- **Follow Up**: Integrate these benefit-driven statements into your overall value proposition to illustrate the real-life advantages of using your product.

[**Crafting the Value Proposition**] - **Objective**: Create a clear and engaging value proposition statement.
- **Prompt**: "Compose a value proposition statement for our new smartphone that emphasizes its cutting-edge camera technology and user benefits."
- **Sample Output**: "Capture life's every detail with exceptional clarity and creativity, thanks to our smartphone's pioneering camera technology— designed for the photographer in everyone."
- **Follow Up**: Test the effectiveness of this value proposition with potential customers to gauge its resonance and refine it based on the feedback received.
By executing these ChatGPT prompts, you will gain:

- A clear identification of what makes your product unique, shining a light on the features that set it apart from others on the market.
- Insight into who is most likely to benefit from and be excited by your product, allowing you to focus your marketing efforts and connect with your audience effectively.
- The ability to translate technical specifications into relatable benefits, making it easier for customers to understand why they need your product in their lives.
- A comparative perspective between your product and its competitors, which can boost your confidence in what you're offering and can also refine your approach to the market.
- A well-crafted value proposition that encapsulates the essence of your product in a way that speaks directly to potential buyers, increasing the likelihood of captivating and retaining their interest.

Airbnb revolutionized the traditional lodging industry by keenly observing the existing market and identifying unmet consumer needs. It saw that travelers were seeking more than just a place to stay; they wanted unique experiences, often at a cost lower than traditional hotels. The strategy hinged on harnessing underutilized private properties and transforming them into short-term rental spaces. This was a market research masterstroke that combined economic pragmatism with a keen understanding of the changing tides in consumer behavior.

Utilizing ChatGPT, one can dissect such strategies by analyzing consumer trends, preferences, and pain points within various market niches. For instance, ChatGPT can help to map the frequency of certain complaints or desires expressed across platforms from social networks to review sites. It can also reveal the gaps between what consumers demand and what they are being offered, just as Airbnb found with the craving for authenticity in lodging.

In addition, ChatGPT can help in evaluating potential partners, tapping into local insights, and even forecasting the ripple effects of regulatory changes. When applied to different industries, such as culinary experiences or transportation solutions, ChatGPT assists in unraveling the complex fabric of user satisfaction and demand patterns, helping companies to innovate with precision—matching solutions to actual human needs.

In this way, ChatGPT becomes an invaluable ally in illuminating the path to service innovation, guiding businesses towards decisions that are not just reactive, but predictive and proactive, much like Airbnb's agile pivot which shook the foundations of the hotel industry.

Start with identifying the core service offering of boutique hotels and define what sets them apart from standard accommodations. This forms the foundation of the market gap analysis. The unique selling points of boutique hotels might revolve around personalized service, local artistry, or thematic stays.

Next, gather data on customer preferences and experiences in the lodging sector. Use ChatGPT to analyze customer reviews and ratings from various platforms, aggregating common praises and complaints. Data synthesis is key here; categorize feedback under different aspects like amenities, aesthetic, location relevance, and service quality.

Analyze competitor strategies by prompting ChatGPT to survey the marketing initiatives, promotions, and partnerships of other boutique hotels and accommodations. Pay attention to strategies that have received social approval for innovation or guest satisfaction.

Proceed to outline current industry trends by examining reports and statistical data on the hospitality sector. Spot patterns in pricing, occupancy rates, and seasonal fluctuations. ChatGPT assists in processing this data to extract trend insights relevant to the boutique sector.

Identify the unmet needs and underserved markets in the hospitality industry similar to what Airbnb discovered, such as affordable stay options that offer a unique local experience. Inquire about rising travel demographics and emergent preference paradigms such as eco-tourism or workations (work vacations).

Formulate potential service innovations by translating identified gaps into new offerings. For example, if there's a high demand for cultural immersion experiences, consider designing stays that include local tours and workshops.

Finally, build a strategic action plan by piecing together your findings into a coherent strategy. Emphasize how the changes or additions to services will fill the gaps in the current market. For boutique hotels, this strategy may involve highlighting unique experiences, partnering with local artisans, or offering immersive packages that big hotels or even Airbnb cannot.

ChatGPT shapes as the analysis tool through each step, allowing for articulation of complex data points into digestible, actionable business insights. The entire process culminates in a tailored approach for boutique hotels to compete in the modern, experience-driven economy.

Jeff Bezos's strategy to place the customer at the heart of every decision catalyzed Amazon's rise from an online bookstore to a global retail titan. This customer-first mindset meant obsessing over providing the best service, price, and selection. It involved listening to customer feedback and letting their needs and desires drive innovation and service improvement.

Translating this ethos into any business starts with understanding customers as deeply as Amazon does. Here, ChatGPT can function as a dynamic tool for gaining these insights. Through prompt-driven conversations with ChatGPT, businesses can analyze customer sentiment, personalize interactions, and automate responses to inquiries with the customer's perspective in mind.

Beyond customer service, ChatGPT can aid in product development by sifting through customer reviews to determine which features are most valued and what areas need enhancement. This relentless focus on the customer experience aligns companies with Bezos's philosophy, central to staying competitive in today's fast-changing marketplace.

Let's take a deeper look at constructing a customer feedback loop with ChatGPT, a process intrinsically designed to elevate a business's customer-centricity to the level exemplified by Amazon. Starting with collection, ChatGPT can be prompted to engage with customers via surveys or direct interactions, capturing their feedback on various aspects of a product or a service. This step is like gathering raw ingredients for a recipe; every opinion carries flavors that, when combined, reflect the overall taste of customer satisfaction.

Moving to analysis, ChatGPT, like a skilled analyst, sifts through responses to detect patterns, sentiments, and recurring themes. The AI interprets the data, separating notable feedback from the noise, highlighting both praises and grievances. It turns a mosaic of individual feedback into a clear picture of overall customer experience.

The actionable revision phase is where things get interesting. ChatGPT helps to brainstorm potential solutions for issues uncovered during the analysis or to enhance features that customers love. This can involve generating ideas for new product features, tweaking service protocols, or identifying areas for staff training.

Implementing these revisions closes the loop and begins a new cycle of feedback collection, ensuring the business evolves in stride with its customer base. Each iteration of this loop, facilitated by ChatGPT, refines the product or service offering, mirroring Amazon's philosophy of perpetual bettoration aimed at exceeding customer expectations.

Envision ChatGPT as the master strategist in a war room, not with maps strewn across tables, but with data points and market trends lining digital screens. The business owner, much like a general, stands ready to deploy their resources most effectively. Here's how ChatGPT could fortify their strategic arsenal:

- "Identify the high ground" – ChatGPT analyzes market data to highlight where the business can capitalize on its strengths, similar to a general seizing a vantage point.
- "Understand the terrain" – Using sentiment analysis, ChatGPT maps the consumer landscape, providing insights into customer needs and competitor moves as a scout reports on the lay of the land.
- "Supply lines assessment" – It helps ensure the business's supply chain is robust and adaptable, mirroring how a general ensures their troops' supply lines are secure.
- "Espionage" – ChatGPT could perform a competitive analysis, akin to spies gathering intel, to inform the business of rivals' strategies and weaknesses.
- "Morale check" – It might gauge brand sentiment and employee engagement, ensuring the company's "troops" are motivated and public favor is strong.

Each scenario leverages ChatGPT's capabilities to give the business leader a comprehensive view of the battlefield, enabling them to make decisions that are not mere shots in the dark but strategic moves crafted from a blend of AI-powered wisdom and human insight.

Here are some ChatGPT prompts designed to strategize market engagement:

[**Market Strength Positioning**] - **Objective**: Find where the business strengths match current market trends.
- **Prompt**: "Identify current market trends where our business strengths can provide a competitive advantage."
- **Sample Output**: "Trends such as personalized customer experience and eco-friendly products are growing, areas where our business has already made

significant strides."
- **Follow Up**: Align business strategies to further develop and market these strengths in response to the identified trends.

[**Sentiment Terrain Analysis**] - **Objective**: Get a detailed overview of customer sentiment about your brand and products.
- **Prompt**: "Conduct a sentiment analysis on customer reviews for our latest product release."
- **Sample Output**: "Customer sentiment is generally positive regarding the product's ease of use and design, but negative around the customer service experience."
- **Follow Up**: Use this feedback to improve the customer service approach and highlight the positive aspects in marketing campaigns.

[**Supply Chain Resilience Review**] - **Objective**: Strengthen the business's supply chain to mitigate potential risks.
- **Prompt**: "Analyze the current supply chain for potential vulnerabilities and suggest improvements."
- **Sample Output**: "The supply chain analysis revealed over-reliance on single-source suppliers and recommended diversification to mitigate the risk."
- **Follow Up**: Investigate alternative suppliers and develop a plan for supply chain diversification.

[**Competitive Strategy Analysis**] - **Objective**: Understand successful strategies of competitors to inform your own.
- **Prompt**: "Present a breakdown of the most effective strategies employed by our top three competitors in the last year."
- **Sample Output**: "Competitors have found success with aggressive social media marketing and partnerships with micro-influencers in niche markets."
- **Follow Up**: Explore potential social media partnerships and assess the feasibility of an influencer marketing campaign for your business.

[**Internal and External Sentiment Measurement**] - **Objective**: Evaluate the internal team morale and external brand perception.
- **Prompt**: "Gauge the current sentiment towards our company both from within the team and from our customers."
- **Sample Output**: "Internal feedback is largely positive with suggestions

for more team-building activities; external sentiment is skewed towards concerns about product durability."

- **Follow Up**: Plan team-building initiatives and address product durability concerns in R&D or quality assurance processes.

[**Innovation Gap Identification**] - **Objective**: Identify underserved areas in the market that present opportunities for innovation.

- **Prompt**: "Analyze current customer feedback across our industry to pinpoint unmet needs and opportunities for product innovation."

- **Sample Output**: "Customers frequently mention the desire for more customizable options in our product category, indicating an opportunity for a tailored product line."

- **Follow Up**: Consider developing a pilot project for a customizable product feature and gather direct customer input on its design.

[**Customer Journey Mapping**] - **Objective**: Understand the path your customers take from discovery to purchase and beyond.

- **Prompt**: "Map out the customer journey for our primary product line, highlighting key touchpoints that influence purchasing decisions."

- **Sample Output**: "The customer journey map shows that online reviews and influencer endorsements are crucial touchpoints leading to a purchase."

- **Follow Up**: Strengthen your online presence through targeted influencer partnerships and encourage satisfied customers to share their experiences online.

[**Price Elasticity Testing**] - **Objective**: Determine the sensitivity of your customers to price changes.

- **Prompt**: "Conduct a price elasticity analysis for our products to see how varying price levels affect sales volume."

- **Sample Output**: "The analysis suggests that there is a moderate degree of elasticity; sales volume decreases when prices increase by more than 10%."

- **Follow Up**: Evaluate pricing strategy to find the optimal balance between affordability for customers and profitability for the business.

[**Brand Positioning Exercise**] - **Objective**: Clearly define how your brand is differentiated from competitors.

- **Prompt**: "Define our brand's unique positioning statement that captures our core values and what sets us apart in the marketplace."

- **Sample Output**: "Our brand is positioned as an eco-conscious choice in the industry, offering innovative, sustainable solutions with a minimal environmental footprint."

- **Follow Up**: Revise marketing materials to consistently reflect this positioning and evaluate how current operations align with these brand values.

[**Promotional Strategy Effectiveness**] - **Objective**: Assess the impact of recent promotional campaigns on sales and brand engagement.
- **Prompt**: "Evaluate the effectiveness of our latest promotional campaign in terms of sales increase and customer engagement."
- **Sample Output**: "The campaign led to a 15% increase in sales and significantly higher engagement on social media during the promotion period."
- **Follow Up**: Look for patterns in the campaign's success to inform future marketing initiatives and replicate effective strategies.

[**Cultural Trend Analysis**] - **Objective**: Leverage cultural trends to inform product development and marketing.
- **Prompt**: "Identify current cultural trends that align with our brand and can be incorporated into our product development and marketing strategies."
- **Sample Output**: "Sustainability and mindfulness are trending. These can be integrated into our brand through eco-friendly products and promoting wellness."
- **Follow Up**: Initiate product development brainstorming sessions focusing on these cultural trends and plan corresponding marketing campaigns.

By executing these prompts, you're essentially gathering valuable intelligence on different aspects of your business environment. Think of it like putting together a detailed map that gives you the lay of the land in high resolution. You'll gain insights into the hidden needs and desires of your customers, often resulting in opportunities for innovation that you can harness. By understanding the customer journey, you're plotting the paths your customers tread, which helps in smoothing their way to your products. Testing price sensitivity equips you with the knowledge to tweak your pricing strategy finely, just like turning the dials for the perfect volume. Clarifying your brand's unique position in the market is akin to planting your flag on a hill where everyone can see it. Finally, measuring the effectiveness of your promotions lets you know if your message is reaching your audience and how they're responding, similar to sending out a beacon and watching for the signals that bounce back.

Executing all the prompts, you will have:

- Identified areas where your business strengths align with market opportunities.
- Gained an understanding of how customers perceive your brand and their sentiment towards your products.
- Strengthened the resilience of your supply chain and identified potential vulnerabilities.
- Gathered competitive intelligence to inform your strategy and find areas where you can outmaneuver the competition.
- Evaluated your company's morale and brand sentiment to ensure a positive internal and external company image.
- Pinpointed underserved areas in the market ripe for innovation.
- Mapped out the customer journey to hone in on key touchpoints.
- Determined how sensitive your customers are to price changes.
- Defined your brand's unique position in the marketplace.
- Assessed the impact of your promotional strategies on sales and customer engagement.
- Leverage current cultural trends to enhance product development and marketing efforts.

ChatGPT stands as a significant ally in the realm of market research, equipping business leaders with the acumen to unravel complex market dynamics and emerging consumer trends. Its transformative power lies in the ability to swiftly process vast amounts of data, discern patterns, and uncover the nuanced preferences of customers. By harnessing this tool, one can step into the marketplace with a measured confidence, armed with intelligence that is both broad in scope and rich in detail. Such empowerment fosters not only a reactive stance to unfolding developments but also a proactive approach, where strategic decisions are informed, foresightful, and grounded in data. In closing, ChatGPT is more than a technological asset; it's a strategic advantage for any business willing to dive into its capabilities, ensuring you are well-prepared to navigate the competitive tides of your industry with poise and informed assurance.

BRANDING AND MARKETING STRATEGIES WITH CHAT GPT

In the fast-evolving landscape of digital marketing, the integration of AI tools like ChatGPT has become a pivotal turning point. This chapter initiates the conversation about how ChatGPT can be harnessed to elevate branding and marketing strategies, infusing traditional concepts with data-driven insight and interactive engagement. ChatGPT's ability to analyze trends, consumer behaviors, and market sentiments equips today's businesses with the agility to craft messages that not only resonate with their audience but also adapt to the ever-changing digital ecosystem. The essence of this chapter is to demystify the application of ChatGPT in practical scenarios, offering clear examples and actionable advice for incorporating AI into your marketing playbook. As you read on, you'll gain the knowledge to use ChatGPT not just as a tool, but as an integral component of your strategy, enhancing the creativity and efficiency of your brand's digital narrative.

ChatGPT's role in analyzing data and informing marketing strategies is akin to that of an experienced market researcher with the added speed and scalability of artificial intelligence. Imagine a scenario where a business aims to understand what drives consumer interest in a particular product. ChatGPT can swiftly sift through vast quantities of consumer feedback, from online reviews to social media conversations, to identify common themes and sentiments. It processes this data using natural language understanding, which allows it to interpret the subtleties of human language, much like a linguist who can detect the mood and preferences expressed in various communications.

Once this information is compiled, ChatGPT employs algorithms – a set of rules for solving problems – to discern patterns that might not be immediately obvious. For example, it might uncover that customers frequently praise the durability of a product, a detail that can inform an ad campaign highlighting this strength. In simpler terms, you can think of ChatGPT as a highly efficient assistant that reads through all the customer feedback you'd ever received, condenses it into key points, and presents these insights in an easily actionable form.

This capability enables marketers to make informed decisions on how to position their product, what messages to focus on in their marketing materials, and even how to improve the product itself. The precision of ChatGPT's analysis helps to avoid guesswork in strategy planning, allowing for strategies that are designed with the customer's voice in mind. As a reader delves into this topic, they will understand how this sophisticated technology can be a cornerstone in building marketing strategies that are not only effective but also deeply rooted in what consumers genuinely want and need.

Step 1: Data Collection

Begin by gathering a comprehensive set of customer feedback. This can come from a variety of sources, including online reviews, social media comments, customer support transcripts, and survey responses. Think of it in the same way a journalist collects information for a story – by pulling together different viewpoints to get the complete picture.

Step 2: Data Preparation

Organize the collected feedback. This involves cleaning the data by removing any irrelevant information, correcting misspellings, and standardizing language for consistency. It's similar to an editor refining a draft before publication, ensuring the content is clear and ready for analysis.

Step 3: Data Input

Input the prepared data into ChatGPT. The AI will process this data, just as a chef adds ingredients to a stew – everything needs to go in before the cooking can start.

Step 4: Natural Language Understanding

ChatGPT uses natural language processing (NLP) algorithms to analyze the feedback. NLP allows ChatGPT to understand human language nuances, like sentiment and context. Picture an expert cryptographer decoding a message – extracting the meaning behind words.

Step 5: Pattern Detection

Using machine learning, ChatGPT identifies patterns and trends within the feedback. Perhaps there's a recurring mention of a product feature that customers love or a service aspect they're dissatisfied with. It's akin to a detective connecting the dots between various pieces of evidence.

Step 6: Insight Extraction

ChatGPT translates these patterns into insights. If customers frequently mention how difficult a product is to use, the reports might suggest focusing on user-friendly design. This step is comparable to an analyst interpreting market signals to forecast financial trends.

Step 7: Strategy Development

ChatGPT uses the insights to recommend marketing strategies. For example, if durability is a highly praised product trait, it might suggest a marketing campaign emphasizing that quality. Imagine a strategist selecting the best course of action based on the intelligence gathered.

Step 8: Actionable Output

Receive a list of actionable items from ChatGPT. This could include revising ad copy, highlighting certain product benefits, or making changes to the product itself. Much like a coach crafting a game plan based on the team's strengths and weaknesses, this output is tailored to what the 'team' (the product or service) does best.

Each step narrows the focus from broad data to specific recommendations, ensuring the marketing strategy is built on the foundation of real customer opinions. You now have a detailed map, not only showing where you stand, but also where to go next.

Crafting a brand identity with the aid of ChatGPT is much like creating a signature dish in the culinary world. Just as a chef selects ingredients with care, aiming to blend flavors in a way that will delight and surprise the palate, a business uses ChatGPT to mix the defining elements of its brand into a coherent identity. The mission statement, like the base flavor of a dish, sets the underlying tone; values add depth and complexity akin to spice layers; visual elements act as the garnish, presenting the brand to the world. ChatGPT assists in refining these ingredients, ensuring they combine harmoniously, much as a sous chef tastes and tweaks, ensuring every element comes through. Imagine a bite of this signature dish that tells the diner a story, much as a strong brand identity resonates with its audience – a unique blend that stands out in a crowded marketplace. With ChatGPT, businesses can discover the essence of their brand narrative, perfecting it until it's ready to be served up to the world, memorable and distinctive.

Let's take a deeper look at the meticulous process of refining a brand's mission statement with ChatGPT's assistance. The initial step involves asking ChatGPT to provide a baseline analysis of the current mission statement, scrutinizing it for clarity, impact, and alignment with the brand's core activities and values. Imagine this as laying all the ingredients on the counter before baking a cake - it's important to ensure that each one complements the other and is necessary for the recipe.

Next, we input this data into ChatGPT to solicit feedback on language, tone, and resonance. ChatGPT examines each word and phrase as if sifting flour to remove lumps, ensuring the message is as smooth and cohesive as possible. The AI highlights parts of the mission that strongly communicate the brand's goals and suggests alterations where the message may not be as effective.

Following this, we engage in an iterative process. Using the feedback, we adjust the mission statement, reframing, adding, or removing elements much like tweaking a recipe after tasting the mix. Each iteration is fed back into ChatGPT, which applies its natural language processing capabilities anew to review the changes – a cycle akin to taste-testing after each adjustment to ensure the flavor profile is just right.

Through successive refinements, ChatGPT helps us solidify a mission statement that clearly conveys the brand's intent and ethos, as if perfecting the layers of flavor in a gourmet dish. The statement must resonate with both the internal stakeholders, ensuring it is representative and motivational, as well as with the consumers, confidently communicating the brand's purpose and promise.

The final mission statement that emerges from this process is a distilled essence of the brand's identity, similar to reducing a sauce to its richest, most flavorful form. This statement becomes the guiding star for all brand activities, ensuring that messaging is uniform across all platforms and resonates with the audience's expectations and the brand's vision. Throughout this journey, ChatGPT acts as the expert guide, simplifying the complex task of brand messaging into an easily navigable and enjoyable endeavor.

Creating a unique value proposition with ChatGPT is akin to visiting a master tailor for a custom suit. First, like taking precise measurements, ChatGPT collects detailed data about a company's strengths and customer needs to ensure a perfect fit. This input acts as the client's unique measurements, detailing not just size but style preferences and the occasions for which the suit is intended.

Next, just as a skilled tailor selects fabrics that complement the client's complexion and stature, ChatGPT helps a business choose words and phrases that best represent its benefits and appeal to its target audience. It's about finding the right material—the company's key features—that will make the suit—here, the value proposition—stand out.

Then, as a tailor crafts a suit to emphasize the best features of the wearer, ChatGPT assists in shaping the value proposition to highlight the company's standout offerings. It cuts and sews the raw material of ideas into a tailored message that drapes elegantly over the contours of the brand's identity.

Finally, just as a tailor ensures the suit fits impeccably and looks remarkable from every angle, ChatGPT fine-tunes the proposition, ensuring clarity and resonance from the customer's perspective. The result? A value proposition that fits the brand like a bespoke suit, perfectly cut and designed to showcase its best features, leaving a lasting impression on anyone who sees it. This process is not just about covering the basics—it's about creating a message so distinct and well-fitted that it elevates the entire brand, just as a bespoke suit elevates one's presence in a room.

Here is the breakdown of the step-by-step process used by ChatGPT to develop a company's unique value proposition:

- **Data Collection**
    - Compile customer feedback from diverse sources, such as surveys, reviews, and social media.
    - Gather internal insights about the company's products, services, and past marketing efforts.

- **Data Analysis**
    - Utilize language models to process natural language data.
    - Identify recurring themes, sentiments, and language patterns within the

collected feedback.

- Isolate specific phrases or statements that resonate strongly with customers.

- Value Proposition Drafting

- Generate a series of potential value proposition statements using the insights from the data analysis.

- Evaluate the emotional impact of each draft and its alignment with the company's brand identity.

- Refinement Process

- Test different drafts of the value proposition with target audience samples, if possible.

- Refine language, tone, and message based on audience feedback and ChatGPT's linguistic analysis.

- Focus on clarity, conciseness, and the power to differentiate the brand.

- Integration with Marketing Strategy

- Align the chosen value proposition with the company's overall marketing strategy.

- Ensure consistency across various marketing channels and materials.

- Prepare the final text of the value proposition for launch in marketing campaigns.

- Presentation and Deployment

- Present the new value proposition internally to align all stakeholders.

- Integrate the value proposition into brand assets, including websites, brochures, and advertising copy.

- Deploy marketing campaigns that spotlight the crafted value proposition to the target audience.

Each of these steps encapsulates critical components of the value proposition development, ensuring that the final message is not only a reflection of the company's strengths but also echoes the voice of the customer. By systematically addressing each element, ChatGPT helps build a value proposition that strikes a chord with consumers and bolsters the company's market position. The goal is not merely to create a statement but to weave a narrative thread that runs through every fiber of the brand's communication, resulting in a cohesive and compelling market presence.

ChatGPT segments an audience as meticulously as a cartographer drafting a map of a diverse landscape. The process begins with data acquisition, akin to surveying the terrain. ChatGPT gathers vast amounts of information on consumer behaviors, preferences, and demographics, drawing from social media activity, purchase histories, and direct feedback.

With this data in hand, ChatGPT begins the segmentation, akin to a cartographer outlining distinct regions on a map. It employs data clustering techniques, sorting individuals into groups based on shared characteristics, much like distinguishing between mountains, valleys, and plains. Through this, the AI distinguishes audience segments, each characterized by unique attributes — some driven by price, others by quality, convenience, or brand loyalty.

The refinement of these segments follows. ChatGPT then fine-tunes the distinguishing features of each group through iterative analysis, which entails reviewing and revising the groupings to ensure precision. It is as if the cartographer zooms in on each area to mark out towns, roads, and rivers, ensuring every detail is captured accurately.

Finally, ChatGPT aligns the distinct audience segments with tailored messaging and marketing strategies. This guide details actionable insights, similar to providing travelers with a map designed for their specific journey, whether they intend to explore the bustling cities (targeting a tech-savvy segment), enjoy the scenic routes (appealing to environmentally-conscious customers), or venture off the beaten path (addressing niche markets with unique desires).

This systematic approach transitions effortlessly from sweeping data landscapes to sharply defined audience topographies. As a result, a business equipped with these detailed audience maps can navigate the market with greater confidence, each step and decision informed by the rich knowledge of their clientele's varied territories.

Here is the breakdown of data clustering techniques that ChatGPT might use for audience segmentation:

- Initial Data Collection
- Assembling consumer data from interactions, transactions, and feedback.
- Mining social media and website analytics for behavioral patterns.

- Data Preprocessing
- Cleaning data to remove inconsistencies and noise.
- Normalizing data to ensure uniform scale across different metrics.

- Feature Selection
- Identifying key variables that influence consumer behavior such as age, location, purchase history, and product preferences.

- Choosing a Clustering Algorithm
- ChatGPT can apply algorithms such as K-means, Hierarchical clustering, or DBSCAN, each suitable for different types of data sets.
- **K-means**: Segmenting data into a predefined number of clusters based on feature similarity.
- **Hierarchical clustering**: Creating a tree of cluster relationships, allowing viewing at various levels of granularity.
- **DBSCAN**: Identifying high-density areas and expanding clusters from them.

- Executing the Clustering Process
- Running the selected algorithm on the data set to form initial groupings.
- Iterating to adjust the clustering parameters for better results.

- Analyzing and Interpreting Clusters
- Evaluating the clusters to understand common attributes within each group.
- Labeling each cluster to reflect its defining characteristics (e.g., 'Budget-conscious young adults', 'Tech-savvy early adopters').

- Optimization and Refinement
- Assessing cluster cohesion and separation to ensure distinct

segmentation.
   - Fine-tuning the clustering parameters like the number of clusters or distance metrics.

   - **Integration with Marketing Strategy**
   - Tailoring marketing messages to align with each segment's attributes and preferences.
   - Deploying targeted campaigns with the expectation of higher engagement.

The goal of these techniques is to achieve clear, actionable segmentation that empowers a business to communicate effectively with different audiences. Through these steps, ChatGPT helps to transform raw data into a map of market segments, each marked by distinct boundaries and characteristics. This clarity offers a foundation on which to build a finely tuned, resonant marketing strategy.

Effective content marketing, much like tending to a garden, requires careful planning and the right nurturing to flourish. Envision ChatGPT as the knowledgeable gardener, selecting the perfect seeds - these are the budding content ideas that have the potential to grow into something substantial and engaging. Just as a gardener evaluates the quality of the seeds, considering factors like the season and soil, ChatGPT assesses the relevance and potential impact of content ideas based on current trends and audience needs.

When the seeds are sown, the focus shifts to nurturing them. This is where ChatGPT helps curate and craft the content, similar to the way a gardener tends to young plants — watering, providing nutrients, and ensuring they have everything they need to grow. In the realm of content, this translates to finessing the language, ensuring the tone resonates with the intended audience, and the message is clear and compelling.

Finally, as a plant reaches for the sun to bloom, content reaches for the audience to achieve its purpose. ChatGPT plays the role of the trellis, guiding and supporting the content's journey toward the light of visibility. It aids in identifying the best channels and strategies to connect with the audience and optimizes content for discovery, much like positioning a plant to get ample sunlight.

In this carefully tended garden, content ideas ultimately flower into valuable pieces that attract and engage. Each piece of content is a blossom, displaying its vibrant colors and unique shape, drawing in those who will appreciate and nurture them in return. Through this analogy, the parallels between gardening and content marketing highlight a process that is both an art and a science, requiring patience, expertise, and the careful touch of a green thumb, or in this case, the digital savvy of ChatGPT.

Let's take a deeper look at how the iterative content refinement process unfolds with ChatGPT at the helm. When ChatGPT assesses content, it essentially puts on an editor's hat, examining a draft for clarity, engagement, relevance, and impact. The goal here is to ensure that the content not only grabs attention but also holds it, much like how an intriguing book compels a reader to turn the page.

This process begins with an initial review, where algorithms evaluate the content against specific criteria: readability, grammar, and tailored language for the intended audience. Imagine ChatGPT with a checklist, ticking off boxes, ensuring the content is easily digestible, linguistically sound, and stylistically on point for its readers.

Next, come the refinement loops. Here, ChatGPT might suggest changes to the structure or diction, fine-tuning phrases to amplify persuasive power or adjusting the tone to better connect with the target demographic. This is a back-and-forth, similar to a writer revising a poem, each word weighed carefully for rhythm and resonance.

Under the hood, sophisticated algorithms enable this refining engine. Language models, trained on vast corpora of text, generate alternatives and suggestions that might better convey the desired message. Sentiment analysis tools weigh in, ensuring the content evokes the intended emotional response from the audience.

From there, ChatGPT can even simulate how different audience segments might receive the content. It's like a focus group, but faster and more exhaustive, testing phrases and passages, then iterating based on feedback—automated but strikingly human-like in curating a piece that resonates.

Finally, the optimization for audience engagement relies heavily on SEO tools and predictive analytics, determining how likely a piece of content is to rank well in search engines or spark interactions on social media. Keywords, title tags, and meta descriptions are scrutinized and selected to align closely with what the audience is searching for—ensuring that when someone looks for the sun, so to speak, they find this content waiting for them.

Each step is critical, interwoven to elevate the content's potential. With ChatGPT's insights, content creators can refine their work to a high polish, clear in its purpose, and compelling in its narrative, ready to meet and engage the audience in the vast digital landscape.

ChatGPT boosts the precision and effectiveness of digital advertising by meticulously combing through past campaign performance. Begin with data collection: ChatGPT takes a close look at various metrics such as click-through rates, conversion rates, and engagement levels, akin to a watchmaker inspecting the gears of a timepiece. It examines which ads performed well, which ones didn't, and explores possible reasons behind these outcomes.

This AI then moves to pattern recognition, identifying successful facets of high-performing ads. Perhaps it's the wording of the call-to-action, the color scheme, or the time of day the ads were displayed. Imagine an analyst spotting trends in a complex graph; ChatGPT operates similarly, but with the capacity to analyze data on a much larger scale.

With these insights, ChatGPT enters the refinement stage. It suggests alterations based on the observed patterns—tweaking ad copy, design elements, or targeting parameters. Think of a chef adjusting a recipe after taste-testing, adding a pinch of salt or a dash of spice to enhance the dish.

Next comes predictive analysis. ChatGPT doesn't just react to past data; it anticipates future trends. Using predictive models, it forecasts how these suggested improvements could lead to better results in future campaigns. In this sense, ChatGPT is akin to a meteorologist using past weather patterns to predict tomorrow's conditions.

Finally, ChatGPT advises on optimization. It may recommend

reallocating the budget to the most promising ads or suggest A/B testing to refine the approach further, resembling a financial advisor suggesting investments based on performance projections.

This process, detailed and systematic, paves the way for more targeted and compelling advertising campaigns. With ChatGPT's help, businesses can continue to adapt and evolve their digital advertising strategies, always aiming for that sweet spot of maximum return on investment and customer engagement.

ChatGPT optimizes digital advertising campaigns using a methodical approach to data analysis and predictive modeling. The process starts with identifying key performance indicators (KPIs) such as click-through rates (CTR), conversion rates, cost per acquisition (CPA), and engagement metrics. These indicators are the pulse points of a campaign's health, similar to how vital signs reflect the state of the human body.

The initial step involves aggregating and organizing the campaign data. This stage resembles a library archivist cataloging books so that the right information can be pulled quickly and efficiently. ChatGPT combs through the data, cleansing it of inconsistencies and grouping related metrics together for a clear comparison.

With the data prepared, ChatGPT then applies statistical analysis to pinpoint patterns and correlations. For instance, it may reveal that a higher CTR correlates with ads displayed during certain hours. This part of the process is akin to a detective sifting through clues and identifying which leads to pursue.

Building on these correlations, ChatGPT next employs machine learning algorithms to delve into predictive modeling. These algorithms can range from regression models that forecast campaign outcomes based on certain input variables to more complex neural networks that can identify non-linear relationships within the data. It's analogous to financial analysts using market trends to predict stock performance.

ChatGPT examines various models, fine-tuning and validating them against a subset of historical data to determine their accuracy. It's much like a scientist experimentally testing hypotheses to verify their findings before making a conclusion.

Once a reliable model is established, ChatGPT simulates potential changes to the campaign parameters within this model to predict outcomes. This can be likened to flight simulators preparing pilots for different flying conditions; ChatGPT similarly prepares marketers for the vast possibilities in digital campaigns.

The final step sees these predictions distilled into actionable strategies. ChatGPT might suggest adjusting the bid for certain keywords, revising ad creatives, or shifting the focus towards higher-performing channels. These suggestions are akin to a coach adjusting team strategies at halftime based on the opponent's performance.

Through each meticulous step, ChatGPT streamlines the advertising process, ensuring that each decision is backed by data-driven insights. This way, marketers can approach their campaign with a plan that is not only reflective of past successes but also adapts dynamically to forecasted trends, keeping their strategy ever relevant and effective in the digital advertising space.

Approach refining your marketing strategies with ChatGPT as if you were a craftsman honing a skill, where each prompt guides you through a part of the process to chisel away imperfections and reveal a more polished plan. Start with a prompt that asks ChatGPT to assess the current effectiveness of your marketing strategies, such as "Analyze the performance data of my last three marketing campaigns and suggest which metrics indicate the highest level of customer engagement."

Once you have insights on past performances, the next prompt could be about identifying weaknesses, like "Identify the least effective aspects of my most recent campaign based on engagement data." This step focuses your attention on what components may require reworking.

For the subsequent prompt, direct ChatGPT to generate suggestions for improvement by asking, "What are some ways I could enhance the visual appeal and message clarity of my social media ads to increase engagement rates?"

Continue the iterative cycle with a prompt that asks the AI to propose experimental changes, such as "Suggest A/B testing scenarios for different headlines and call-to-actions to determine which combinations resonate the most with my audience."

As you review these insights, refine your strategies further with prompts that delve into deeper analysis, like "Based on successful competitors, what content strategies could we adopt to improve our brand's online presence?"

The final prompt could be about measuring potential success, asking ChatGPT, "If we implement the suggested content strategies, what predictions can be made about our customer engagement growth over the next quarter?"

By engaging with these prompts, you involve yourself in an ongoing, evolving dialogue with ChatGPT, where each question and answer takes you one step closer to a marketing strategy that not only performs but excels. Each iteration is like passing a piece of rough wood to a finer grain of sandpaper; with every pass, you remove the coarse edges, gradually revealing a smooth, polished surface. This process encourages a mentality of constant learning and adaptation, essential for navigating the competitive currents of the market.

Here are some ChatGPT prompts that revolve around refining marketing strategies through detailed analysis and optimization steps:

[**Initial Campaign Analysis**] - **Objective**: To evaluate the performance of past marketing efforts and identify strong elements worth replicating.
- **Prompt**: 'Analyze the performance data from my last three marketing campaigns, focusing on engagement metrics, and provide a breakdown of the most effective elements.'
- **Sample Output**: 'Analyzing the provided data, it appears that campaigns featuring user testimonials and clear call-to-action buttons have the highest engagement rates...'
- **Follow Up**: Consider amplifying these successful elements in upcoming campaigns and observe if the engagement rates continue to trend positively.

[Weakness Identification] - **Objective**: To pinpoint and understand areas of the marketing campaign that underperformed.
- **Prompt**: 'Identify the least effective aspects of my latest marketing campaign by examining the customer interaction and drop-off points.'
- **Sample Output**: "The analysis shows a significant drop-off rate on the landing page with the current product video...'
- **Follow Up**: Revise the underperforming content, such as redesigning the landing page or reworking the product video, and re-evaluate their effectiveness in the next campaign iteration.

[Visual and Message Clarity Enhancement] - **Objective**: To enhance the appeal of marketing visuals and message for better engagement.
- **Prompt**: 'How can I improve the visual elements and clarity of the messaging in my social media ads to drive higher engagement?'
- **Sample Output**: "To boost engagement, consider using high-contrast colors for your call-to-action button and simplify the ad copy for immediate comprehension...'
- **Follow Up**: Implement these suggestions in a small set of ads and measure the changes in engagement levels to verify the effectiveness of the adjustments.

[A/B Testing Design] - **Objective**: To create a structured approach for testing variations in ad components.
- **Prompt**: 'Design a set of A/B tests for optimizing headlines and call-to-actions in my social media ads.'
- **Sample Output**: 'For your A/B tests, compare headlines that lead with benefits versus features, and test call-to-action phrases...'
- **Follow Up**: Carry out the A/B tests as per the design, analyze the results, and implement the most successful elements more broadly.

[Competitive Strategy Adoption] - **Objective**: To explore effective content strategies used by competitors and adapt them for personal use.
- **Prompt**: 'Based on the content strategies employed by top competitors, which practices should we consider adopting to improve our marketing?'
- **Sample Output**: "Top competitors are seeing great engagement from storytelling in their content. Incorporating narratives that resonate with your audience could be beneficial...'
- **Follow Up**: Develop content incorporating these storytelling elements and monitor key performance metrics to assess the impact on engagement.

[**Engagement Metrics Focused Improvements**] - **Objective**: To refine specific marketing content based on engagement metrics analysis.

- **Prompt**: 'What changes can be made to my marketing content to improve likes, shares, and comments according to the latest engagement metrics?'

- **Sample Output**: 'To enhance engagement, consider incorporating interactive elements such as polls, or asking direct questions to encourage audience participation...'

- **Follow Up**: Implement the suggested interactive elements in your next set of social media posts and track any changes in engagement metrics to evaluate the impact.

[**Re-targeting Strategy Formulation**] - **Objective**: To develop a re-targeting strategy aiming to recapture the interest of users who have previously engaged with the brand.

- **Prompt**: 'Formulate a re-targeting strategy for users who have visited our website but did not make a purchase.'

- **Sample Output**: 'To re-engage website visitors, set up a re-targeting ad campaign showing them personalized offers or products they viewed but didn't purchase, and use persuasive copy...'

- **Follow Up**: Implement the re-targeting strategy and analyze the return on ad spend (ROAS) to determine the strategy's profitability and effectiveness.

[**Optimizing Content for SEO**] - **Objective**: To improve the search engine visibility of marketing content.

- **Prompt**: 'Advise on how I can optimize my content for better SEO results highlighting the most impactful ranking factors.'

- **Sample Output**: 'Focus on optimizing title tags, meta descriptions, and including high-quality, relevant keywords within your content to improve SEO rankings...'

- **Follow Up**: Update your content with the suggested SEO enhancements, monitor changes in search rankings, and adjust your strategy based on results over time.

[**Social Media Time Slot Analysis**] - **Objective**: To identify the optimal times for posting on social media for maximum user engagement.

- **Prompt**: 'Analyze my social media engagement data to determine the best days of the week and times of day to post our content.'

- **Sample Output**: 'Based on your engagement data, posting on Tuesday afternoons and Thursday evenings yields higher interaction from your audience...'

- **Follow Up**: Adjust your posting schedule based on these findings and measure whether engagement rates improve during these suggested time slots.

[**Customer Journey Mapping**] - **Objective**: To gain insights into the typical path a customer takes from discovery to purchase and optimize marketing efforts accordingly.

- **Prompt**: 'Map out the customer journey for our core product line and identify touchpoints where marketing efforts can be enhanced or added.'

- **Sample Output**: 'Customers typically discover your product via social media ads, then visit review sites before purchasing. Consider increasing ad frequency and partnering with review platforms...'

- **Follow Up**: Streamline your marketing strategy to strengthen the identified touchpoints, and then analyze conversion rates to see if the changes lead to improved sales.

By executing these prompts, you gain a meticulously crafted compass to navigate the intricacies of marketing strategies. It's about transforming raw data into actionable insights, similar to transforming unshaped clay into a sculpted masterpiece. Each prompt serves as a step in this process, guiding you to extract the essence of past performance, finetune current practices, and forecast future outcomes. This hands-on exploration with ChatGPT is like having a dialogue with a digital marketing consultant, one that responds to your specific needs and nudges you toward a clear understanding of what works and what doesn't. Ultimately, you'll cultivate a marketing strategy that's not just based on intuition but reinforced by data-backed decisions.

By executing these prompts, specifically, we have:

- Identified key performance indicators to guide our future marketing efforts.

- Isolated and addressed weaknesses in our current marketing strategies.

- Enhanced the visual and textual appeal of our social media advertisements.

- Designed and implemented A/B tests to determine the most effective ad elements.

- Analyzed and adopted successful strategies from competitors to improve our approaches.

- Forecasted the potential success of our updated content strategies in engaging customers.

- Identified the optimal posting times for social media content for greater

user engagement.
- Mapped the customer journey to understand and optimize the key interaction points.

These steps, put together, craft a robust framework for our continually evolving marketing strategy.

ChatGPT dissects social media trends and engagement metrics with the keen eye of a data analyst. This AI delves into patterns of likes, shares, and comments to understand what content resonates with audiences. Picture a scientist observing reactions to stimuli; similarly, ChatGPT evaluates how users interact with different types of posts, stories, and campaigns. It scrutinizes metrics like peak engagement times, demographic details, and sentiment scores, piecing together a digital puzzle that, when solved, paints a picture of audience preferences.

Using these insights, ChatGPT crafts strategies designed to amplify marketing messages. It can suggest the tone, timing, and topics that are most likely to spark interest and drive engagement on social media platforms. For instance, if video content garners more attention, ChatGPT might recommend focusing on rich media posts. It's akin to a coach developing a game plan based on the opposing team's weaknesses—except the 'opponent' here is audience apathy.

Beyond engaging content, ChatGPT also assesses conversational threads, lending insights into how a brand might forge stronger customer relationships. It points out opportunities for meaningful interactions—prompting when it might be beneficial to respond to comments, seek out user feedback, or initiate community-driven discussions.

By orchestrating these elements, ChatGPT equips you with a multifaceted strategy that not only projects marketing messages further into the digital sphere but also nurtures a proximity with customers, much like a shepherd tends to their flock, ensuring none stray too far from the fold. This process marries analytical prowess with a crafted approach to communication, ensuring that every social media move is a calculated step towards building a loyal and engaged community.

ChatGPT steps into the world of social media data analysis by first gathering the raw data, much like how a collector might begin with gathering artifacts for curation. This data encompass metrics such as likes, shares, comments, and the reach of various posts across platforms. To extract this data efficiently, ChatGPT may tap into APIs provided by each social media platform, pulling in numbers and textual data for analysis.

Moving on, ChatGPT acts as a processor, categorizing this data to make sense of it. It sifts through the information for patterns: What time were people most active? What content types—videos, images, articles—resonated most? This is akin to preparing ingredients for cooking; each needs to be prepped and evaluated for quality before use.

The next part involves identifying key metrics for engagement. ChatGPT looks for what captured audience interest—high engagement figures such as shares might indicate content that viewers felt worth spreading, for instance. It also considers metrics like sentiment analysis drawn from comments, which reveal the audience's emotional response.

With a sound understanding of what sparks engagement, ChatGPT steps into the role of a strategist, developing communication tactics designed to fuse with the identified trends. If GIFs at noon brought a spike in interactions, the strategy might include more of such posts around that time. It is similar to planning a menu after learning guests' favorite dishes.

The sophistication is in the details—ChatGPT may propose personalized responses to common queries in comments, fostering a relationship much as a local shopkeeper might remember regulars' names and preferences. In this phase, ChatGPT is less about automating responses and more about providing a framework for genuine conversation.

The final piece involves looping this process as an ongoing cycle. As ChatGPT provides these insights and strategies, they are tested in real-time, with subsequent data feeding back into the system for the next round of analysis. Imagine a gardener adjusting care for each plant based on how they responded to watering or sunlight; similarly, your social media strategy adjusts and evolves over time.

In essence, ChatGPT helps you understand your audience's digital landscape, allowing you to plan your routes (content and strategies) that will most likely lead to meaningful customer engagements and relationships. It takes complex data and turns it into a road map for success in the ever-shifting world of social media marketing.

Think of ChatGPT as a skilled artisan in the workshop of marketing, equipped to craft promotional concepts with the allure of a Steve Jobs keynote or the narrative depth of a Nike advertisement. Just as Jobs captivated audiences with a masterful blend of anticipation and reveal—a magician with a penchant for technological wonder—ChatGPT can analyze his speeches, pinpointing patterns of engagement, rhetoric, and stagecraft to generate promotional concepts that capture that same spellbinding effect.

Crafting a narrative as compelling as Nike's storytelling ads, on the other hand, is like weaving a rich tapestry, with threads that each tell a part of a greater human story. ChatGPT can delve into the fabric of Nike's successful campaigns, extracting the essence of their emotionally charged stories that resonate with the aspirations and dedication of athletes around the world. It then uses these insights to sew together promotional narratives that echo with the beats of inspiration and determination.

In recreating this magic, ChatGPT merges the analytic with the artistic, using algorithms as its paintbrush and data as its palette. The end result is a suite of promotional concepts that resonate with the characteristics that made Jobs' presentations legendary and Nike's ads iconic—an orchestra of words and ideas that play a symphony appealing to both the emotions and intellect of the audience. It's a process that not only respects the original maestros but also adapts their harmony into new, unique compositions that speak clearly to our current age, carrying a chorus of innovative celebration and raw, heartfelt storytelling.

Here is the breakdown on how ChatGPT could dissect elements from Steve Jobs' keynotes and Nike's advertising campaigns:

- **Analyzing Steve Jobs' Keynotes**
  - Speech Patterns
    - Capturing the rhythm and pacing of Jobs' language.
    - Extracting signature phrases or sentence structures that create suspense and reveal.
  - Presentation Techniques
    - Identifying the use of pauses for emphasis and audience engagement.

- Noting the visuals that complement the spoken word, like product reveals and demonstrations.
- Emotional Resonance
- Mapping the emotional journey of the keynote, from anticipation to excitement.
- Assessing the use of storytelling to create a personal connection with the audience.

- Understanding Nike's Storytelling Ads
- Narrative Structure
- Breaking down the beginning, middle, and end of Nike ads to understand how they construct compelling stories.
- Analyzing the challenges, triumphs, and resolutions featured in the narratives.
- Visual and Audio Elements
- Cataloging the types of imagery and music that bolster the storyline.
- Detailing camera work and editing styles that enhance the emotional impact.

- Formulating Promotional Concepts
- Synthesis of Elements
- Merging the key findings from Jobs' keynotes and Nike's ads to develop new promotional angles.
- Creating concept pitches that encapsulate identified successful strategies, adapted for different products or services.
- Campaign Development
- Crafting messages that build up to a product reveal in the spirit of Jobs' presentations.
- Developing story-driven content that aligns a product or service with the customer's journey, inspired by Nike's commercials.

The aim is to employ ChatGPT's capabilities to mine through iconic marketing material and sculpt promotional concepts that echo the mastery of Jobs' charisma and Nike's narrative savvy. It involves a detailed unpacking and creative reconstruction of what made those approaches successful, and how those techniques can be used to craft new, enchanting marketing narratives for today's audience. This process is a testament to the importance of both analysis and creativity in marketing, offering a blueprint for how AI can complement human ingenuity.

ChatGPT stands as a powerful ally in the realms of branding and marketing, its capabilities marking a significant shift in how professionals approach the digital landscape's challenges. Equipped with the ability to analyze vast data streams, predict market trends, and craft tailored content, this AI tool empowers you to make data-informed decisions to engage and expand your audience. Each feature, from language analysis to sentiment understanding, is a lever in your control, fine-tuning your brand's voice and narrative to resonate with today's consumers.

You now possess the understanding to wield ChatGPT in augmenting your branding efforts, ensuring that your strategies are not only innovative but also grounded in the nuances of consumer interaction. With ChatGPT, you are prepared to craft experiences that are both personal and impactful, ensuring your brand's message cuts through the noise and reaches the hearts and minds of your audience. This newfound preparedness is less about following a well-trodden path and more about forging your path with confidence, wielding a toolset that is both versatile and insightful.

SALES OPTIMIZATION AND CUSTOMER SERVICE ENHANCEMENT

In the digital marketplace, mastery of sales optimization and customer service is a powerful advantage—a key unlocking potential growth and customer loyalty. This chapter lays bare the process of refining sales funnels and invigorating service experiences, tools that collectively hold the power to transform a business's outreach and client relations. Sales optimization streamlines the journey from lead to customer, simplifying and speeding up transactions. Simultaneously, enhancing customer service guarantees that every client interaction adds value, turns support scenarios into opportunities for brand advocacy, and cements long-term relationships. These practices are essential, not peripheral, shaping the modern approach to business in a world where customer expectations are ever-evolving. With this knowledge, you gain more than strategies; you equip yourself with a blueprint for sustainable success in an online world where every customer interaction counts.

Imagine your sales funnel as the family kitchen sieve, the one that's seen countless recipes come to life. Just as this kitchen staple is trusted to separate the wheat from the chaff, so too does the sales funnel separate the fleeting passersby from genuine potential clients. Picture your marketing efforts much like a gentle rain of water, showering down into the sieve. Some droplets hastily rush through without a second thought, akin to casual visitors with passing interest. Yet, those droplets that linger, that find themselves caught within the mesh—are the leads that hold promise, the ones that are ideally suited for what your brand has to offer. It's these precious caught droplets that you'll carefully nurture and usher through to conversion, each one a delicate blend of interest and opportunity, ready to be turned into a lasting client relationship. This, right in the heart of the home—the kitchen— is where potential transforms into loyalty, much like ingredients meld into a beloved family dish.

Let's take a deeper look at the lead nurturing process within the sales funnel. This intricate yet imperative procedure involves cultivating potential clients with the finesse of a gardener tending to a seedling. It begins with the initial contact, where potential leads are greeted with a personalized message tailored to their interests—a strategy that echoes the personalized welcome of a small-town shopkeeper.

Then, communication continues steadily, resembling the regular watering of plants. This might take the form of insightful emails, informative blog posts, or engaging social media content, all aimed at providing value to the potential client and deepening their interest in the brand.

As leads progress through the funnel, engagement grows more robust. At this stage, strategies resemble a chef seasoning a dish to perfection. Techniques include targeted offers based on past interactions, personalized product recommendations, or invitations to exclusive webinars. It's about enriching the relationship and establishing trust.

To measure the success of these efforts, specific metrics come into play—analogous to a farmer assessing crop health. Metrics like email open rates, click-through rates on content, and conversion rates offer insight into the quality of the leads and how well they're responding to nurturing efforts. High levels of engagement and positive responses to calls-to-action are telltale signs of high-quality leads, indicating a readiness to bloom into loyal customers.

By meticulously attending to these details, the nurturing process guides potential leads to the point of conversion—where interest translates into action, and action translates into sales. It's a delicate balance of providing value, building relationships, and steadily guiding leads to that decisive moment of purchase, ensuring that by the time they reach the end of the funnel, they don't just emerge as customers, but as brand advocates. This thorough care taken at every step not only fortifies consumer connections but also secures a healthy, vibrant business growth.

AI plays a pivotal role in refining the sales funnel, similar to how a jeweler meticulously shapes and polishes each facet of a gem. At the start of the funnel, think of AI, like ChatGPT, as the analyst that examines vast streams of consumer data. It identifies personal preferences and behaviors, allowing for interactions to be custom-tailored, ensuring that each prospective client feels understood, much as a bespoke suit fits perfectly to its owner.

Further along the funnel, AI continues to refine the process by anticipating needs. Just as a seasoned gardener can spot early signs of plant stress, AI predicts potential drop-off points for leads. It analyzes patterns of interaction—or lack thereof—and proactively suggests interventions to retain lead interest. This could mean offering a well-timed discount or a piece of content that addresses their specific hesitations.

By the funnel's end, the goal is conversion, and here AI ensures a seamless transition. In the way an experienced pilot navigates through turbulence to ensure passengers hardly feel a bump, AI smooths out the purchasing process, potentially automating payment procedures or streamlining user interfaces for effortless transactions.

Articulating the mechanisms of AI in the sales process sheds light on a detailed, interconnected system designed to enhance the customer journey at every step. The sophistication of AI lies not just in its data processing capabilities but in the human-like intuition it brings to digital interactions, bridging the gap between businesses and their customers with precision and personal touch. This understanding equips the reader with a more nuanced perspective on the digital sales and marketing world, empowering with knowledge that transcends the purely technical, and resonates with the practicalities of growing a business in today's digital economy.

AI employs a range of algorithms to refine each stage of the sales funnel, functioning much like a team of experts. At the top of the funnel, where potential leads are identified, AI uses data mining techniques. This is comparable to a miner sifting through soil to find precious metals; the AI sifts through social media activity, web browsing patterns, and purchase histories to unearth leads with the highest potential for conversion.

Once potential leads are identified, machine learning algorithms step in to personalize interactions. Imagine a bespoke clothing tailor crafting an outfit based on individual measurements. Similarly, the AI analyzes past interactions and uses predictive analytics to forecast what content or products might interest a customer, then adapts messaging to suit their preferences.

As leads move through the funnel, patterns in their engagement or sudden changes in behavior—like a drop in website visits or email opens—are fed into decision trees and logistic regression models. These are akin to checkpoints a doctor uses to diagnose patients; if certain symptoms or signs are present, it indicates the patient may need intervention. In the sales funnel, such signs may trigger automated emails with discounts or personalized content to re-engage the lead.

The funnel's endgame is conversion. Here, the AI optimizes the checkout process, ensuring ease much in the way a skilled guide facilitates a smooth passage through difficult terrain. The systems in place work behind the scenes to facilitate transactions, from suggesting alternative products based on availability to automating payment processing procedures, creating a seamless experience.

Throughout the journey, the AI constantly learns and improves its functions, embodying a methodological analysis and improvement process similar to a scientist conducting experiments and refining hypotheses. This continuous loop enhances the AI's ability to predict behaviors, tailor experiences, and ultimately, increase conversion rates. The technical prowess of AI is not just in calculating probabilities or processing heaps of data; it's in translating this data into a language of personalized customer service that feels intuitively human, fostering a connection that encourages leads to become loyal customers.

Consider the transformative power of a simple smile: it can turn a momentary encounter into a repeat visit. In a similar vein, customer service becomes the cornerstone in transforming casual browsers into loyal customers when it is underscored by responsiveness and personalization. AI tools, such as ChatGPT, serve as the backbone for this transformation. They act much like the attentive store clerk who not only greets customers but remembers their last purchase and suggests products they might like.

At its core, this service is facilitated by ChatGPT examining previous customer interactions—data points that include purchase history, product preferences, and communication styles. Armed with this knowledge, it can personalize future communications, tailoring suggestions and support to each individual. AI's ability to respond quickly and accurately to customer inquiries mirrors a concierge promptly fulfilling a guest's request, enhancing satisfaction.

Breaking down the process, AI-supported customer service begins with the collection of customer data, progresses to the analysis of patterns and preferences, and culminates in the execution of tailored responses. It is in these nuanced, seemingly small gestures of understanding customer needs that loyalty is cemented.

The true sophistication of such technology is found in the details—how it discerns the tone of customer feedback or how it predicts future needs based on past behavior. However, it is also important to note the limitations: AI can guide and improve the customer service experience, but it does not replace the genuine human connections that characterize the very best of customer relationships. Through this lens of understanding, one can appreciate how AI like ChatGPT reinforces the fabric of customer service, positioning businesses to not only meet but exceed the evolving expectations of their clients.

Let's take a deeper look at the specific AI methodologies applied in the realm of customer relationship management. At the heart of these processes is the collection and analysis of customer data. AI systems function like meticulous record-keepers, tracking each customer interaction, purchase, and feedback response. These 'records' are chunks of data that, when aggregated, form a comprehensive customer profile.

From there, natural language processing, a specialized AI branch, steps in to parse customer communication. Imagine it as a linguist deciphering languages. It not only picks up on what is said but also how it's said, noting nuances in sentiment and intent. This subtle discernment allows AI to gauge customer satisfaction and tailor future conversations.

Predictive analytics is another cog in the machinery. Comparable to a weather station forecasting conditions, these analytics use historical data to predict future behaviors. For example, if a customer frequently checks prices for a specific item, AI may forecast an intent to purchase and flag this for a timely promo offer to that customer.

Machine learning algorithms continuously refine these processes. Picture a craftsman sharpening tools; as the machine learning model is fed more data, it sharpens its accuracy in personalizing communications and offers. Over time, the AI can start to recognize patterns that indicate, say, an increased likelihood of a customer considering a competitor. It can trigger interventions, sending tailored deals or product recommendations to keep the customer engaged.

Each AI task reinforces a company's ability to understand and serve its customers in a manner that feels unique and personal. By absorbing and interpreting vast amounts of data, AI constructs a virtual 'persona' of each customer, aligning service more closely with each one's expectations and preferences. This meticulous process not only enhances the present customer journey but also shapes a more predictive and responsive model for future interactions, ultimately fostering a tight-knit relationship between business and customer.

Picture ChatGPT as a digital concierge, a tireless assistant who is always on duty, ready to engage customers with the swiftness and attention to detail akin to that of staff at an upscale hotel. This technology facilitates conversations in real-time, much like a concierge listens to guests and provides instant responses. For product recommendations, ChatGPT peers into its vast repository of information—the digital equivalent of a concierge's local knowledge—and suggests options that align with the customer's past preferences and inquiries.

When it comes to service issues, ChatGPT operates with the efficiency of a seasoned hotel butler, swiftly addressing concerns and finding solutions. The AI sifts through customer service tickets, categorizes them, and employs its learned experience from previous interactions to resolve them, or escalates them with all necessary context to the appropriate human expert.

Behind this seamless interaction are complex algorithms that interpret the customer's language, sentiment, and underlying needs. Like the gears of a well-oiled clock, these algorithms work in unison to provide a service that feels both personal and immediate. ChatGPT doesn't sleep, doesn't take breaks; it's the ever-present support that businesses and customers can rely on at any moment.

Yet, for all its sophistication, ChatGPT isn't a replacement for human touch—it's an enhancement to it. It provides the technical backbone that supports and amplifies the empathetic, nuanced service that only human staff can deliver. With ChatGPT, the wisdom and warmth of human service blend with the speed and efficiency of AI, ensuring that every customer interaction is as effective and pleasant as possible. This partnership of human and digital concierge redefines customer service excellence, heralding a new era where every digital interaction bears the hallmark of five-star treatment.

Here are some ChatGPT prompts that revolve around enhancing customer service and personalization using AI:

Here are some ChatGPT prompts that revolve around enhancing customer service and personalization using AI:

[Instant Customer Engagement] - **Objective**: To simulate how AI can engage customers instantly and intelligently.
- **Prompt**: 'As an AI digital concierge, initiate a conversation with a customer who has just entered the online store, greeting them and asking if they need assistance with any specific products.'
- **Sample Output**: 'Hello! Welcome to our online store. If you're looking for something specific today or need recommendations, I'm here to help you find exactly what you need!'
- **Follow Up**: Analyze the interaction to assess the effectiveness of the AI's opening and its ability to encourage further engagement.

[Product Recommendation Tailoring] - **Objective**: To personalize the shopping experience through AI-driven product suggestions.
- **Prompt**: 'Given a customer's purchase history of skincare products, generate a list of personalized recommendations with reasons for each choice.'
- **Sample Output**: 'Based on your previous purchases, I recommend our hydrating serum for your dry skin concerns, and since you bought sunscreen, you may also like our new SPF-infused day cream!'
- **Follow Up**: Review the recommendations to ensure they align with the customer's history and interests, and consider offering a tailored discount for the suggested products.

[Service Issue Resolution] - **Objective**: To resolve common customer service issues rapidly and satisfactorily.
- **Prompt**: 'As AI customer support, draft a response to a customer reporting a delayed delivery for their recent order.'
- **Sample Output**: 'I understand your order hasn't arrived as expected, and I apologize for the inconvenience. I'm checking the status and will update you promptly with the new estimated delivery time.'
- **Follow Up**: Look into the customer's order details and provide a realistic updated timeframe or alternative compensation.

[Sentiment Analysis Feedback] - **Objective**: To analyze customer feedback for underlying sentiments and improve service accordingly.

- **Prompt**: 'Perform a sentiment analysis on the following customer review and respond appropriately to acknowledge the feelings expressed.'
- **Sample Output**: 'Thank you for your feedback. It's great to hear you loved the product's quality, and I understand the packaging didn't meet your expectations. Your input is valuable, and we're looking into packaging improvements.'
- **Follow Up**: Identify areas for improvement based on the analysis and plan how to implement changes in the business, such as upgrading packaging.

[**AI and Human Agent Interaction**] - **Objective**: To show how AI can facilitate a handover to a human agent for complex issues.
- **Prompt**: 'If a customer presents a complex issue requiring a human touch, demonstrate how you as AI would involve a human colleague.'
- **Sample Output**: 'I've noted the complexity of your issue and to best assist you, I'm transferring you to one of our experienced human agents, who will be better suited to handle this unique situation.'
- **Follow Up**: Evaluate the transition process including customer satisfaction and the time taken for the human agent to resolve the issue post-transfer.

By executing these ChatGPT prompts, you will gain:

- A practical understanding of how AI can provide real-time customer service, much like an attentive in-store employee, enhancing the immediacy and quality of your customer interactions.
- Insight into the processes of AI-driven product recommendation systems and the nuanced way they can match products to a customer's history and behavior, leading to a more personalized shopping experience.
- Experience in dealing with common customer service scenarios, learning how AI can address and resolve issues rapidly to maintain high customer satisfaction.
- Skills in sentiment analysis, enabling you to interpret and effectively respond to the emotional content of customer feedback and reviews, which is critical for reputation management and customer relations.
- Knowledge of the handover process from AI to human customer service agents, ensuring complex issues are resolved with a personal touch, promoting a seamless service experience.
- An appreciation for the balance between automated efficiency and human warmth, understanding how combining AI with human service can create a comprehensive and responsive customer service model.

Each of these gains contributes to a holistic strategy that uses technology to foster strong customer relationships, drive sales, and improve overall service quality. As each facet is mastered, you'll be equipped to implement a customer service approach that aligns with the needs and expectations of modern consumers.

Consider Amazon as a colossal ocean liner, with its sales processes and customer care as the navigational systems that guide it through the unpredictable retail seascape. Just as a captain uses a compass, maps, and a seasoned crew to ensure a vessel's steady passage amidst the tempest, Amazon fine-tunes its colossal operation with data-driven precision—its compass. The retailer's vast analytics act as the stars by which it charts its course, ensuring that each customer interaction is as smooth and efficient as the ship slicing through the waves.

The commitment to customer care is akin to a dedicated crew, ready to respond to any challenge that the ocean throws their way. When a customer encounters a problem, Amazon's customer care swoops in much like the swift response of a crew member, ensuring that the issue is resolved, and the journey remains comfortable for all aboard. These meticulously calibrated elements come together to create a seamless journey, emulating the grace with which a well-commandeered ship traverses even the most daunting of waves, confirming that Amazon doesn't merely float; it sails with purpose and direction.

Here is the breakdown of Amazon's data analytics and customer service processes:

- **Data Collection**
   - Customer Interactions: Every click, purchase, and search on Amazon's platform is recorded.
   - Feedback Systems: Amazon gathers input from customer reviews and star ratings.

- **Data Analysis**
   - Predictive Analytics: Using past behavior to anticipate future needs.
   - Machine Learning Algorithms: Constantly learning from new data to improve predictions and recommendations.

- **Customer Interaction Personalization**

- Product Recommendations: Based on browsing and purchase history, tailored suggestions are made.
- Targeted Advertising: Ads are personalized to align with customers' interests.

- Customer Service Operations
- Automated Responses: Chatbots provide instant answers to frequently asked questions.
- Issue Resolution: Customer service tickets are categorized and addressed based on priority and content.

- Order Fulfillment and Delivery
- Logistics Optimization: Data analytics streamline the route and delivery processes.
- Inventory Management: Anticipating demand to ensure product availability.

- Customer Relationship Management (CRM)
- Customer Profiles: Detailed records of customer behavior, preferences, and purchase history.
- Engagement Tracking: Monitoring customer interaction frequency and quality.

- Customer Feedback Loop
- Post-Purchase Surveys: Gathering insights into the customer's buying experience.
- Continuous Improvement: Adjusting operations based on customer feedback data.

Through this meticulous process, Amazon ensures that operations run efficiently and customer satisfaction remains high. Each component plays a critical role, from collecting the vast data that enables personalized shopping experiences to using feedback for constant enhancement of service quality. Just as a skilled craftsman uses tools to shape their creation, Amazon wields data and customer feedback to sculpt an industry-leading service experience.

ChatGPT handles the complexity of consumer data much like a master chef orchestrates a symphony of flavors in a high-end culinary masterpiece.

Just as the chef selects ingredients with purpose, ensuring each complements and enhances the other, ChatGPT sifts through customer demographics, previous buying behavior, and current market trends. It takes this blend of information, analyzing and combining it, to compile promotional campaigns that appeal to consumers' unique tastes and preferences.

The method involves dissecting vast amounts of data to identify patterns – recognizing, for instance, that customers who bought a certain product often searched for related items. From these insights, ChatGPT crafts messages designed to strike a chord with its audience, akin to how the perfect balance of sweet and savory can delight the palate.

This isn't about casting a wide net; it's targeted culinary artistry at its finest, tailored to leave a memorable impression on those it's designed to reach. Yet, one must recognize the limitations; just as even the most thoughtful dish may not suit everyone's taste, so too might some promotions resonate less with certain audiences. Nevertheless, equipped with ChatGPT's refined approach to data, the resulting campaigns are poised to captivate a majority, harmonizing the science of analysis with the art of consumer attraction.

Here are some MetaPrompts that revolve around creating targeted and personalized marketing campaigns using AI analytics, similar to a master chef crafting a unique culinary experience:

[**Crafting Personalized Offers**] - **Objective**: To leverage consumer data and create personalized offers that engage customers and drive sales.
- **ChatGPT MetaPrompt**: 'Generate prompts that will instruct ChatGPT to analyze customer purchase history and behavior to create custom discount offers for an e-commerce clothing brand.'
- **Expected Output**: A list of prompts that result in tailored discount offers, loyalty rewards, or exclusive product previews based on individual customer data.
- **Follow Up**: Use these generated prompts to create real customer offers and track engagement to measure the effectiveness of targeted campaigning.

[**Identifying Buying Patterns**] - **Objective**: To pinpoint consumer buying patterns for better stock management and tailored recommendations.
- **ChatGPT MetaPrompt**: 'Create a series of prompts that instruct ChatGPT to identify products frequently bought together within a home

goods online retailer.'

- **Expected Output**: Prompts that lead to analytical insights on product combinations and the formulation of bundle deals or recommendations for future product development.

- **Follow Up**: Implement insights from the responses into marketing strategies to upsell related products and optimize inventory.

[**Segmenting Customer Demographics**] - **Objective**: To segment customers effectively based on demographics to improve the relevance of marketing campaigns.

- **ChatGPT MetaPrompt**: 'Develop prompts for ChatGPT that utilize demographic data to segment customers into target groups for a marketing campaign of a new sports drink.'

- **Expected Output**: Prompts that instruct ChatGPT to divide a customer base into specific groups based on factors like age, location, and fitness levels.

- **Follow Up**: Employ the segments identified to tailor marketing material for each group and monitor campaign performance across different demographic segments.

[**Tuning Marketing Tone**] - **Objective**: To align the tone of marketing messages with customer sentiment and brand identity.

- **ChatGPT MetaPrompt**: 'Compose prompts for ChatGPT to create multiple versions of marketing copy that match different customer sentiment profiles for a tech gadget launch.'

- **Expected Output**: A set of prompts that direct ChatGPT to craft specialized marketing copy that ranges from friendly and casual to professional and technical based on customer sentiment.

- **Follow Up**: Test different versions of the marketing copy with respective customer sentiment groups and measure interaction rates to find the most effective tone.

[**Optimizing for Trending Preferences**] - **Objective**: To keep promotions in sync with current trends and customer preferences.

- **ChatGPT MetaPrompt**: 'Design prompts for ChatGPT to generate a weekly updated list of trending topics and interests to include in social media marketing for a beauty brand.'

- **Expected Output**: Prompts that command ChatGPT to scour the web and social media for popular trends in beauty, leading to dynamic and engaging content topics.

- **Follow Up**: Integrate trending topics identified into the brand's social media strategy and assess engagement to refine content curation over time.

By executing these metaprompts, you will gain:

- The ability to mold ChatGPT into a tool that adapts and responds to individual customer data, leading to offers and promotions that reflect each customer's unique interests and buying habits.
- Insights into the relational patterns between products and how they can be used to predict customer behavior, empowering you to create more compelling product bundles and improve inventory management.
- A practical method to classify your customer base into meaningful demographics, providing you a clearer picture of your market segments and the ability to tailor campaigns that resonate more effectively with each group.
- An understanding of how to calibrate the tone of your marketing messages to align with various customer sentiments, enhancing the likelihood of positive reception and engagement.
- Real-time awareness of trending topics and customer preferences, which is crucial for maintaining relevance and dynamism in your social media marketing efforts.
- The opportunity to build a robust feedback loop, using the generated prompts to refine and evolve your marketing strategies, making them data-driven and customer-focused.

Each of these gains will not just enrich your marketing expertise but also provide actionable paths toward elevating your brand's customer engagement and sales effectiveness.

The mastery of sales optimization and customer service stands before us, not as distant peaks to climb but as accessible landscapes to traverse with confidence. Armed with profound insights and innovative tools, the path to amplified client satisfaction and robust business success is now clearly marked. Each stride taken in understanding how to personalize interactions, streamline service, and respond to the needs of a diverse clientele is a step toward enduring success.

Navigating this terrain requires precision—the kind that transforms scattered data into coherent strategies, much like turning individual notes into harmonious symphonies. Every technique, be it harnessing AI for tailored recommendations or analyzing feedback for continuous improvement, is a meticulously chosen step that ensures the journey is as rewarding for customers as it is for the business.

There lies substantial importance in this realm; the caliber of customer service and the agility of sales tactics can distinguish a thriving business from a stagnant one. By adopting these comprehensive approaches to sales and service, one can expect not only to meet customer expectations but to exceed them, fostering loyalty and sparking growth.

View these tools as guides in a dialogue with a customer base—conversations that are meant to be as fruitful as they are revealing. It is in the nuance of personalized service that a business truly resonates with its clientele, and with these newly acquired understandings, such resonance is within reach. This isn't the end of a learning chapter, but the bright beginning of a new way of engaging, an open invitation to keep evolving with customers at the heart of every decision.

OPERATIONAL EFFICIENCY AND AUTOMATION

Stepping into a business that hums with the seamless rhythm of efficiency is a testament to the power of automation. This chapter reveals the transformative effect of ChatGPT on such an environment, where the intricate dance of productivity and process becomes ever more synchronized. Integrating this AI-driven technology refines the workflows with precision, freeing up time and resources that can be redirected towards innovation and growth.

In a system where ChatGPT operates, communication flows unimpeded, schedules align like clockwork, and the once tedious tasks are managed with ease and speed. This isn't a scenario nestled in the distant future; it's a reality that's within reach now. The incorporation of ChatGPT into daily operations carries with it the promise of elevated productivity—an outcome resonating clearly with businesses seeking to maintain their competitive edge.

More than just a tool, ChatGPT is a facilitator of harmony in the workplace, channeling its capabilities to enhance human potential. The value brought by such integration does not lurk in the shadows but shines brightly, highlighting the path towards a more efficient, responsive, and ultimately successful enterprise. With explanations anchored in the practical application of AI, this chapter serves as a guide for anyone looking to understand how to harness the symphony of opportunities that such technology brings.

Operational efficiency occurs when a business functions with the precision and grace of a well-tuned engine. Here, resources are allocated and utilized with intention, mirroring the conservation of energy in a high-performance machine, which uses exactly what is needed—no more, no less—to produce maximum output. This approach to business operations ensures that services or products are delivered with a focus on quality, while unnecessary expenditure of time and effort is minimized.

It involves an ongoing process of evaluation and refinement—much like fine-tuning a musical instrument—to achieve the best possible performance. Each step, from the initial gathering of resources to the final delivery to customers, is scrutinized for efficiency gains and opportunities to cut excess without sacrificing the end result. It is about understanding every component of the business, identifying which parts are crucial and which are superfluous, and optimizing accordingly.

This doesn't just mean doing things quickly; it means doing things smartly so that every action adds value to the end product or service. Implementing such a strategy is synonymous with placing the business on a steadfast path toward not only maintaining a competitive stance in the market but also ensuring long-term viability and success. It's a disciplined, methodical approach that, once mastered, leads to consistent outcomes that customers can rely upon, bolstering both trust and satisfaction.

Let's take a deeper look at the meticulous steps a business can take to audit and refine their operations for maximum efficiency. The process starts with a thorough review, which is akin to a health check-up, assessing all parts to ensure they're working optimally. Here's a step-by-step method employed:

1. **Operational Audit**: Initiate with an operational audit. This includes an in-depth look at current processes to spot any inefficiencies, much like searching for leaks in a pipeline. This is done through interviews with staff, observations, and reviewing process documentation.

2. **Data Collection**: Accumulate data related to these processes. This could involve tracking the time it takes to complete tasks, the resources used, and the costs involved—clear-cut figures that lay the groundwork for analysis.

3. **Performance Metrics Identification**: Choose performance metrics that are pivotal for assessing efficiency. Common ones include throughput, which measures the rate of production, and utilization, indicating how effectively a business uses its resources.

4. **Process Mapping**: Proceed by process mapping, which involves creating a flowchart of all steps in a process. This reveals the workflow visually, showing where delays or redundancies might occur.

5. **Bottleneck Identification**: Look for bottlenecks, the slowest steps that limit throughput. It's like finding where the traffic is heaviest and figuring out a way to ease it.

6. **Lean Techniques Application**: Apply lean techniques such as 5S (Sort, Set in order, Shine, Standardize, Sustain) to organize the workplace and reduce waste. Think of it as decluttering a closet to make finding what you need faster and easier.

7. **Automation Opportunities**: Pinpoint operations that could be automated. If a task is repetitive and rule-based, it's a candidate for automation—similar to how a dishwasher takes over from washing dishes by hand.

8. **Continuous Improvement Cycle**: Embed a continuous improvement cycle using methodologies like PDCA (Plan, Do, Check, Act). It's an ongoing iterative process just like updating your smartphone's software for performance enhancements.

9. **Technology Leverage**: Upgrade to technologies such as ERP systems that integrate all business operations into a single interface, streamlining processes akin to switching from a paper map to a GPS for navigation.

10. **Feedback Loop**: Establish a feedback loop where employees can report issues and suggest improvements. It's like having a suggestion box that continually collects ideas for enhancements.

By approaching each of these steps with a goal of simplification and streamlining, companies can boost their operational efficiency dramatically. The approach isn't about large sweeping changes but often the small, consistent tweaks to processes that together make a substantial impact, ensuring that the company operates smoothly, waste is minimized, and both employees and customers are more satisfied with the outcomes.

Automation emerges as the backbone of modern business, silently and relentlessly tackling tasks that are repetitive and time-consuming. This technology streamlines processes that once consumed hours of manual effort, much like a dishwasher takes over the tedium of hand-washing dishes. By assuming these repetitive duties, automation liberates the workforce, enabling minds to venture beyond the grind of monotonous tasks and delve into the realms of innovation and strategic thinking.

Breaking down this process, automation involves programming machines or software to perform set tasks that follow specific rules, such as data entry or sorting emails. The tools employed — ranging from simple scripts that sort digital files to complex robotic arms assembling products — operate with autonomy, requiring little to no human intervention once set up.

While this technology vastly increases productivity and consistency, it also sheds light on human potential. With automation handling the 'busy work,' employees can apply their unique cognitive skills to areas where human touch makes a difference — problem-solving, customer service, and creative development.

The practical benefits are vast, yet understanding its workings is critical. For instance, automation relies heavily on the quality and structure of the input data — garbage data in, garbage data out. It is also bound by the confines of current technology, which means it may not yet handle tasks requiring nuanced judgement or emotional intelligence.

By navigating through these considerations with care, one can harness automation as a catalyst for business growth. It isn't just about doing more in less time but awakening the full spectrum of human creativity and expertise, propelling the business into a future where technology and human ingenuity work in concert for progress and prosperity.

Let's take a deeper look at the varied spectrum of automation tools and how they are used across different business landscapes. From software that schedules appointments to machines that manage entire manufacturing processes, automation is as diverse as the sectors it serves.

In administrative and office environments, automation often appears as software bots. These digital assistants carry out tasks such as organizing files, managing emails, or entering data. In customer service, they can power chatbots that answer common inquiries, allowing staff to focus on more complex customer needs.

The manufacturing sector employs a different class of automation: physical robots. These can range from robotic arms that assemble components on a production line to autonomous vehicles that transport materials across a factory floor, all driven by complex algorithms that dictate their movements with precision.

Retail, particularly online, harnesses automation in logistics. Algorithms optimize inventory based on real-time sales data, predicting stock needs before a shortage arises. Furthermore, systems automatically route orders to distribution centers and choose delivery paths.

Financial sectors lean on automation for transaction processing, risk assessment models, and even fraud detection—tasks requiring rapid processing of large volumes of structured data, where algorithms excel over manual effort.

The healthcare industry benefits from automation that schedules patient appointments and manages medical records. Automation here not only saves time but also enhances accuracy and privacy in handling sensitive information.

Integrating these tools into current workflows starts with a clear understanding of the tasks they will assume. Define the objective, such as increasing output or reducing error rates, and then choose a tool that best suits the need. Implementation may involve configuring the software, training employees, and setting up monitoring systems to ensure the smooth operation of the new tools.

While these tools offer significant advantages, including increased speed and potential cost savings, they're not without limitations. They require well-defined processes and clean, structured data to work effectively; otherwise, they can produce errors or become inefficient. They also don't replace the need for human judgment, creativity, or decision-making—areas where human intelligence still triumphs.

By meticulously selecting the right tools for the job, fine-tuning them to fit into the orchestration of a business's routine, and appreciating their strengths and boundaries, companies can wield automation not as a replacement for the human workforce, but as a powerful ally to it, enhancing the workplace and pushing the boundaries of what's possible.

Imagine ChatGPT as the newest, shiniest piece in an intricate watch, sliding in to click perfectly with the other components. Just as this cog helps the watch's hands move in rhythmic synchrony, marking time down to the second, ChatGPT integrates into the flow of daily business activities. It takes over tasks that we might think of as the 'background noise' of the workspace—scheduling appointments is as smooth as setting an alarm clock, organizing emails becomes as easy as sorting silverware, and compiling reports is as systematic as following a recipe.

Each function of ChatGPT is like a familiar tool made more efficient: it's the calendar that never double-books, the file organizer that never misplaces a document, and the writer that distills data into concise summaries without hesitation. In the grander scheme of the business world, ChatGPT's role becomes clear—not only does it uphold the productivity by managing the routine, but it also frees up the most valuable asset in any company: the human mind and spirit to engage in creative endeavors. This isn't about replacing human effort but about enhancing it, turning every workday into an opportunity for innovation and every goal into an achievable milestone, all the while maintaining the essential rhythm of efficiency and precision.

Here is the breakdown of ChatGPT's automation features, the programming that powers them, and how they propel human creativity and operational efficiency within businesses:

- **Task Automation**
- Appointment Scheduling: ChatGPT is programmed to recognize calendar inputs, schedule appointments without conflicts, and send reminders.
    - **Benefits**: Reduces double bookings and frees individuals from the calendar management chore, allowing them to engage in more meaningful activities.
- Email Sorting and Response: Utilizes natural language processing to categorize emails and draft replies based on pre-set criteria.
    - **Benefits**: Saves time by prioritizing important communications and

handling routine responses, streamlining the inbox management process.

- Report Generation: Programmed to pull data from various sources, synthesize information, and present it in a structured format.

- **Benefits**: Eliminates hours spent on data compilation, enabling employees to analyze the results and draw conclusions quickly.

- Customer Service Enhancement

- Chatbots for Customer Inquiries: ChatGPT can be tailored to address frequently asked questions and provide instant customer support.

- **Benefits**: Enhances customer satisfaction through immediate responses and allows human agents to focus on complex queries that require empathy and deeper problem-solving.

- Content and Documentation

- Document Drafting: Contains templates for standard documents which it customizes using specific details provided by the user.

- **Benefits**: Streamlines the creation of routine documents, such as invoices or memos, ensuring consistency and accuracy.

- Content Creation: Generates written content for various platforms, adapting style and tone to the intended audience.

- **Benefits**: Supports marketing and content strategies by quickly creating drafts, saving time for creative input and refinement.

- Continuous Learning and Optimization

- Feedback Loops: ChatGPT is built to learn from each interaction and improve the relevance of its responses over time.

- **Benefits**: Continuously improves the accuracy of task automation, providing increasingly valuable support and reducing error rates.

- Customization and Integration: It can be customized to integrate with existing business systems and workflows, enhancing its utility.

- **Benefits**: Aligns with specific operational needs, ensuring that the transition to automation is smooth and adds the most value.

Each component of ChatGPT's robust automation features aims to tackle the repeatable while upholding high standards of output. This allows human talents to be directed towards strategic planning, innovative pursuits, and high-level decision-making—areas inherently reliant on creativity and depth of thought. These automation tools are not an end but a means to elevate the human capacity within the business ecosystem.

Imagine if, on your morning commute through the bustling city, you stumble upon a previously unnoticed shortcut—a serene alley that slices through the chaos, delivering you effortlessly to your destination. This is what it's like when a business embraces ChatGPT. It becomes the secret passage that bypasses the monotonous jam of routine tasks. Suddenly, employees are catapulted to the forefront of innovation and richer customer interactions, far from the everyday gridlock of the mundane.

ChatGPT handles the necessary, yet repetitive, behind-the-scenes business tasks, akin to a silent butler who anticipates needs and discreetly manages the workings of a household. Emails, schedules, customer queries—they're managed with the deftness of a street performer juggling balls, never missing a beat. This frees up the human intellect and spirit to do what it does best—conceive, create and connect on a personal level.

Embracing ChatGPT isn't just about speeding up processes; it's about enhancing the quality and significance of the work, making every minute count towards something truly impactful. It's about unlocking the full potential of a team, unburdened by the routine, to explore, innovate, and forge connections that create enduring value. This isn't merely an upgrade in efficiency—it's an evolution of the workplace itself.

Here is the breakdown of tasks that ChatGPT can automate in a business environment, illuminating how it interfaces with other systems, demonstrates its diverse skills, and upgrades various business processes:

- **Customer Support Automation**
    - Immediate Response Systems: ChatGPT is set up to answer frequently asked questions, delivering instant support to customers.
    - **Interaction**: Integrates with customer relationship management (CRM) software to access client data and personalize interactions.
    - **Capabilities**: Can handle a high volume of queries simultaneously.
    - **Process Enhancement**: Elevates customer satisfaction levels with quick response times and reduces the workload on human support teams.

- **Internal Communication Efficiency**
    - Email Management: It sifts through inboxes, tagging, and routing important emails while drafting and sending responses for common or

repetitive inquiries.

- **Interaction**: Works alongside email clients and adheres to company-specific communication protocols.
- **Capabilities**: Learns from ongoing communication patterns to improve sorting accuracy.
- **Process Enhancement**: Frees staff from email administration, allowing them to concentrate on strategic communication.

- **Administrative Duties Streamlining**
- Schedule and Calendar Management: ChatGPT automates the setting, rescheduling, and canceling of appointments, avoiding conflicts, and optimizing time allocation.
- **Interaction**: Syncs with calendar applications and sends reminders to participants.
- **Capabilities**: Balances and updates multiple calendars with consideration for time zones and availability.
- **Process Enhancement**: Saves administrative time and ensures efficient day-to-day operations.

- **Data Analysis and Reporting**
- Report Generation: Gathers data from various sources, analyzes it according to specified parameters, and compiles comprehensive reports.
- **Interaction**: Integrates with databases and analytics tools to extract and process information.
- **Capabilities**: Translates complex datasets into intelligible insights.
- **Process Enhancement**: Informs decision-making with up-to-date, accurate information, presenting it in an easily digestible format.

- **Content Creation and Management**
- Documentation and Content Writing: Drafts content ranging from business documents to promotional materials, adapting style and tone as needed.
- **Interaction**: Can pull information from content management systems for reference and context.
- **Capabilities**: Generates consistent, high-quality content tailored to business requirements.
- **Process Enhancement**: Accelerates content production cycles and supports marketing strategies.

- **Language Translation and Localization**
  - Multilingual Communication Support: Translates content and communication into different languages to support international operations.
    - **Interaction**: Can work in conjunction with translation memory tools to maintain consistency across documents.
    - **Capabilities**: Broadens communication reach, handling a wide array of languages.
    - **Process Enhancement**: Enables businesses to connect with a diverse, global customer base more effectively.

As a comprehensive AI solution, ChatGPT handles repetitive yet essential tasks with ease, aiding businesses to not only run more smoothly but to also carve out space for human creative thinking and strategic growth. With its potential for continuous learning and adaptability, ChatGPT serves as a dynamic tool in the business toolkit, one that grows in value as it's put to use. The myriad tasks it can take on and the processes it can refine all contribute to a transformed workplace, where efficiency and human creativity achieve a beneficial balance.

Tim Cook and Elon Musk stand as navigators in the realm of business, steering Apple and Tesla, respectively, towards the pinnacle of operational excellence. Their leadership exemplifies a meticulous focus on processes and a passionate commitment to innovation, cornerstones that support the creation of superior products and services. Cook, for instance, deploys a detailed approach to Apple's supply chain management, streamlining operations with pinpoint accuracy to ensure product quality and timely delivery. Similarly, Musk's pursuit of groundbreaking technologies at Tesla and SpaceX underlines the importance of pushing boundaries to achieve remarkable feats in transportation and space exploration.

The methods these leaders use involve layering cutting-edge technology with thorough operational strategies, aligning every business segment from production to customer experience toward a unified goal. Their tactics are less about racing to the finish line and more about calibrating every turn and straightaway for ultimate performance. This kind of granular mastery over business variables transforms companies into benchmarks within their industries.

Despite the intricacy of their roles, both CEOs manage to demystify the complexity of leading edge enterprises, illustrating that, while the path to excellence is demanding, it is navigable with the right mix of foresight, precision, and willingness to venture into uncharted territories. Their strategies offer instructive insights into the power and potential of attentive, forward-thinking leadership—a resonating lesson for anyone aiming to leave a mark in their professional waters.

Let's take a deeper look at the particular operational strategies and innovative measures Tim Cook and Elon Musk have cemented within their respective companies, Apple and Tesla/SpaceX, and unravel how these methods ripple through their industries.

Tim Cook honed Apple's operational efficiency by focusing sharply on the company's supply chain. The meticulous approach includes:

- **Supplier Relationships**: Building strong, collaborative relationships with a wide network of suppliers, ensuring Apple can secure the best materials and components.
    - **Function**: This ensures not just high-quality components but also favorable pricing and prioritization during high-demand periods.

- **Inventory Turnover**: Keeping low inventory levels to minimize holding costs and react more swiftly to market changes.
    - **Function**: It allows Apple to adapt quickly if a product soars in popularity or if technological advancements emerge.

- **Streamlining Production**: Continually seeking ways to automate and refine the manufacturing process to reduce time and increase yield.
    - **Function**: Reduces potential errors and production bottlenecks, leading to a higher standard of product finish.

- **Retail Integration**: Seamlessly integrating online and physical retail experiences to offer unparalleled customer service.
    - **Function**: Provides customers a consistent Apple brand experience, whether shopping online or in-store.

Elon Musk's approach at Tesla and SpaceX revolves around pushing the frontiers of technology:

108

- **Vertical Integration**: Bringing large portions of production in-house to maintain control over the quality and speed of component manufacturing.
- **Function**: Speeds up innovation cycles as design, manufacturing, and assembly occur under one roof, allowing Tesla/SpaceX to fine-tune quickly.

- **Direct-to-Consumer Sales**: Eschewing traditional dealership models to sell vehicles directly to consumers.
- **Function**: Reduces additional costs and enables a closer relationship with customers, providing a richer understanding of consumer needs and feedback.

- **Reusable Rocket Technology**: Innovating with reusable rocket components to drastically cut the cost of space travel.
- **Function**: Makes space travel more sustainable financially and environmentally, setting new industry standards.

Under their leadership, Apple, Tesla, and SpaceX have integrated cutting-edge technology not as an afterthought but as a central pillar of their business strategies, which has led to the development of products and services that redefine market expectations. These strategies have cemented their companies' statuses as leaders, influencing industry standards regarding product quality, customer experience, and sustainable practices. These leaders exemplify that understanding every widget of a process and viewing each with a lens of potential innovation can result not only in excellence but in a legacy of change within the industry.

ChatGPT acts as an analytical coach for your business, meticulously reviewing your company's daily operations akin to how a sports coach analyzes game footage. Armed with the capability to process vast amounts of information, ChatGPT scans through workflows, identifying points where processes slow down or speed up—pinpointing inefficiencies as clearly as a coach spots a missed pass or a successful play.

By examining communication patterns, response times, and task completions, it discerns where the workflow excels and where it lags. With such analysis in hand, one can understand the areas that demand attention— perhaps an approval procedure taking too long, or a step where automation could replace manual labor. Equally, it reveals operational strengths, such as areas with consistently high performance or particularly efficient teams.

This systematic review enables a business to make informed decisions about where to allocate resources, invest in training, or implement new technologies. The aim is not to criticize but to strengthen, taking what works well and making it the norm across the board, while shoring up the spots that are falling behind.

ChatGPT, therefore, is not just a tool for automating tasks but a means for strategic operational enhancement. By recognizing the full spectrum of how it can analyze business operations, one can utilize it to foster continuous improvement, ensuring each part of the business is functioning optimally and contributing to the collective success.

Here are some ChatGPT prompts centered on analyzing and enhancing business operations:

[**Identify Inefficiencies in Workflow**] - **Objective**: To pinpoint areas where the business's workflow is slow, allowing for targeted improvements.
- **Prompt**: 'Analyze the provided workflow data from our sales team and identify which steps take the longest relative to the others.'
- **Sample Output**: 'Based on the analysis, steps 3 and 7 are taking 25% longer than the workflow average, indicating potential inefficiencies in the sales follow-up and deal-closing phases.'
- **Follow Up**: Investigate the causes for delays in these identified steps and consider process changes or training to improve efficiency.

[**Optimize Resource Distribution**] - **Objective**: To adjust resource allocation for streamlined operations and reduced waste.
- **Prompt**: 'Given the recent production and sales figures, recommend how to balance manufacturing output with sales to minimize overproduction.'
- **Sample Output**: 'To reduce overproduction, adjust manufacturing outputs according to the sales forecast trends showing a 15% decrease in demand during Q3.'
- **Follow Up**: Use ChatGPT's recommendations to realign manufacturing plans with projected sales data and track results for any needed adjustments.

[**Enhance Team Productivity**] - **Objective**: To elevate team performance by identifying bottlenecks and proposing solutions.
- **Prompt**: 'Review our project milestone achievements from the past six months and pinpoint which phases are consistently met with delays.'
- **Sample Output**: 'Delays are regularly occurring in the quality assurance phase, leading to subsequent project milestones being missed by an average of two weeks.'
- **Follow Up**: Focus on the quality assurance process, looking at ways to improve testing efficiency or providing additional resources to this phase.

[**Automate Routine Administrative Tasks**] - **Objective**: To free up human resources from repetitive tasks by introducing automation.
- **Prompt**: 'Assess the list of daily administrative tasks completed by the HR team and identify which ones can be automated using current technology.'
- **Sample Output**: 'Tasks such as time tracking, leave requests, and initial candidate screenings are suitable for automation with existing HR management software solutions.'
- **Follow Up**: Look into implementing the suggested software automation for these tasks and monitor the impact on team productivity and employee satisfaction.

[**Improve Customer Service Response**] - **Objective**: To speed up customer service without compromising quality.
- **Prompt**: 'Evaluate our customer service chat logs for response time and quality metrics, and suggest enhancements for both.'
- **Sample Output**: 'There's a noticeable lag in response times during peak hours from 2 pm to 4 pm. Consider automating responses for common queries and redistributing staff schedules to cover peak times more effectively.'
- **Follow Up**: Implement the changes in automation and staffing to see if there's an improvement in response times and customer satisfaction during the identified peak periods.
By executing these ChatGPT prompts, you will gain:

- **Insight into Operational Flow**: A clearer view of how tasks and responsibilities move through your business, revealing the efficiency of each step along the way.
- **Identification of Potential Improvements**: The ability to identify specific areas where your current processes might be slowing down, allowing

111

you to target those areas for improvement that could make your business run smoother and more efficiently.

- **A Roadmap to Enhance Productivity**: Concrete steps to redistribute your valuable resources, be it time, staff, or materials, in a manner that could boost productivity without additional strain on the business.

- **Strategies for Team Empowerment**: Knowledge about which phases in project management need attention and the freedom for your team to focus on more meaningful tasks by automating routine work.

- **Customer Service Enhancements**: Actionable ideas for how to improve customer service, ensuring clients receive timely and quality responses that could enhance the overall customer experience.

- **Data-Driven Decision Making**: The opportunity to make informed decisions with the help of data-driven analysis, minimizing guesswork and enabling strategic changes that are evidence-based.

Each of these gains not only offers the chance to streamline and optimize your business practices but also empowers you to lead your operations with confidence, backed by the insights derived from careful analysis and reflection.

Imagine entering the future of business, a landscape where AI tools like ChatGPT act not as replacement pilots, but as reliable co-pilots to human intellect and creativity. These advanced tools are designed to handle an array of tasks that, while necessary, are not the best use of human talent—like organizing data, scheduling meetings, or generating reports. Just as a dishwasher takes over the task of cleaning up after a meal, these AI assistants tackle the less glamorous work, allowing individuals to focus on creating, strategizing, and innovating.

In this future, ChatGPT does more than just automate—it analyses patterns in vast datasets to inform business decisions, connects seamlessly with various digital systems to ensure smooth workflow, and is constantly learning to perform its tasks more effectively. The innovation doesn't stop with mundane tasks; these tools also offer fresh perspectives on complex problems, providing suggestions that might not be immediately obvious to their human colleagues.

Yet, with all its sophistication, ChatGPT remains a tool—a complement to human reasoning, not a substitute. As with any technology, it has boundaries. It operates within the scope of its programming and the data it receives, which underscores the continuing need for human oversight and intervention. But when used effectively, ChatGPT and similar AI tools can enhance the way businesses operate, making for a work environment that is not just more efficient but also more human-centric, where every team member can engage in work that is truly transformative.

Let's take a closer inspection of the inner workings of AI tools like ChatGPT and how they delve into the sea of data within a company to bring up valuable pearls of insight. These AI systems use a method called natural language processing (NLP) to interpret and understand data in a way that is meaningful. This is akin to a person reading a report and extracting important points, except AI can do this on a much larger scale and at an astonishing speed.

Once these AI tools comprehend the data, they apply machine learning algorithms to detect patterns and correlations that might not be immediately obvious. For example, they might notice that sales of a product spike after certain marketing campaigns, or identify that customer satisfaction drops if response times go above a certain threshold. This is like putting together a puzzle; ChatGPT can ascertain which pieces of information fit together to form a complete picture.

Integrating these AI systems with existing business systems is like giving them the keys to the kingdom. They can tap into databases, access customer relationship management (CRM) systems, and use enterprise resource planning (ERP) tools to not just analyze stand-alone data but to see how data from different sources interacts. This holistic view can inform strategies that cover everything from inventory management to personalized marketing initiatives.

The automation of data analysis through AI tools enhances decision-making by providing accurate, up-to-date information. Instead of waiting for a human analyst to compile a monthly report, AI can deliver real-time insights, enabling businesses to make swift decisions in dynamic market conditions. It effectively allows companies to stay agile, adapting to trends and making nuanced adjustments that keep them ahead of the curve.

Ultimately, employing AI like ChatGPT doesn't just offer a company a snapshot of its current state; it provides a telescope to gaze into the future, predicting outcomes based on current trends. It spotlights the strengths within the operations and gently illuminates areas of potential growth, all while ensuring the human workforce can target their efforts where they're most impactful. With each task that AI automates and every insight it provides, it paves the way for businesses to not only operate more efficiently but to innovate continuously and strategically.

Integrating ChatGPT into business workflows marks a strategic move towards operational excellence. Incorporating this AI isn't merely about keeping pace with digital trends; it signifies a progressive leap to position your company at the vanguard of innovation. Such an enhancement to the operational toolkit translates to every procedure being honed to its finest— eschewing mere survival for a state of thriving.

The adoption of ChatGPT streamlines the minutiae of daily tasks, affording teams the freedom to dedicate more time to substantive, creative pursuits contributing directly to business growth. It's about fine-tuning operations with such dexterity that quality is uncompromised, efficiency is peaked, and productivity blooms. By enabling ChatGPT to absorb routine responsibilities, businesses infuse agility into their structures, ready to respond to ever-evolving market demands with foresight and finesse.

This technological empowerment brings clarity of purpose to each business facet, where every task, no matter how small, is executed with precision and contributes to the overarching mission. In doing so, businesses gain the advantage of foresight, anticipating shifts and skirting obstacles with the ease of an entity that's not just current but pioneering.

DATA ANALYSIS AND DECISION MAKING WITH CHAT GPT

ChatGPT redefines the data analysis landscape for business professionals by offering an unparalleled convenience in sifting through information and drawing conclusions. It's a tool that transforms the vast oceans of data into navigable waters, allowing for more precise and informed decision-making mechanics within businesses. With ChatGPT, data no longer remains just a raw sequence of numbers and words but becomes a clear map to smarter business strategies and outcomes.

Understanding and utilizing ChatGPT for data analysis does not require extensive coding knowledge or a deep background in data science. It's about leveraging this AI-fueled assistant to distill complexities into actionable insights. ChatGPT brings data analysis to every professional's desk, facilitating decisions that are both timely and data-backed.

Deploying ChatGPT means equipping your business with a powerful ally, one that processes information with the attention to detail equivalent to an expert analyst, yet operates with the user-friendliness of a simple office application. This shift towards accessible, AI-driven data interpretation fundamentally changes how strategies are crafted, empowering even those new to data analysis to make informed, confident decisions.

In the realm of data, the distinction between qualitative and quantitative types is foundational. Quantitative data is numerical—it's measured and expressed using numbers, akin to a stopwatch that precisely captures time down to the millisecond. This data type allows for measurement and comparison, such as tracking the number of sales transactions or the hours spent on a task. Qualitative data, on the other hand, is descriptive and often collected through interviews, surveys, or observations—imagine capturing the essence of a customer review, with its opinions and sentiments that a number can't fully convey.

The methods used to collect data are equally critical. A flawed collection process is like trying to fill a bucket with a hole in it; inevitably, some water escapes, just as insights can be lost if data isn't gathered carefully and methodically. Proper collection methods ensure the integrity and accuracy of the data, making it trustworthy for analysis.

Enter ChatGPT, an AI that excels at ordering and interpreting piles of raw data. It organizes quantitative data by identifying trends and patterns, and it can digest qualitative data, such as feedback forms, to extract predominant themes. Think of ChatGPT as a skilled librarian who not only categorizes books by genres but also offers a summary of the themes within the stories. It assists in managing data's complexity, saving professionals from the tedium of manual organization and leaving them with clear, processed information ripe for analysis.

As businesses increasingly rely on data to drive their decisions, understanding these foundational concepts becomes imperative. ChatGPT stands as a powerful ally in this data-driven environment, providing clarity and insight that is crucial for crafting solid, informed strategies. It invites users to approach data with confidence, regardless of their expertise, illuminating paths to advancement and growth.

Let's take a deeper look at how ChatGPT sifts through both quantitative and qualitative data to uncover insights crucial to guiding business decisions. When ChatGPT faces numbers, or quantitative data, it applies statistical methods like regression analysis — which can predict outcomes based on patterns in the data — much like forecasting weather trends by looking at past temperatures. For qualitative data, which encompasses things like customer feedback or interviews, ChatGPT employs natural language processing algorithms. These are sets of rules and techniques designed to understand and interpret human language. Consider this process akin to breaking down the plot of a novel into its key themes and character arcs.

ChatGPT can recognize the sentiment expressed in text, categorize information into themes, and extract relevant entities, such as names and places, similar to how a researcher codes qualitative data by identifying recurring words or phrases. For businesses, this means turning a daunting array of customer opinions into a coherent summary of customer satisfaction drivers or concerns.

Synthesizing these various data strands, ChatGPT brings together the hard facts of numbers with the nuanced context of human language. By doing so, it provides a multifaceted view of the data that informs more holistic business insights — spotlighting not just the 'what' but also the 'why' behind the patterns. This comprehensive analysis can lead to the identification of new market opportunities, refined customer personas, or even product improvements.

In essence, ChatGPT acts as a versatile interpreter that translates raw data into a narrative that business leaders can understand and act upon. The technology takes the complexities of data analysis and presents it as clear, actionable information, empowering even those unfamiliar with data science to make informed decisions that can propel their business forward.

ChatGPT harnesses machine learning to process and analyze data, functioning akin to a savvy detective piecing together clues from a scene. It starts by sifting through vast amounts of raw data, sorting the numerical figures and text through filters that it has learned over countless interactions. Just as a gold panner separates dirt from precious nuggets, ChatGPT discerns trivial data from valuable insights.

For quantitative data, think of ChatGPT as employing a sophisticated calculator, computing statistics and searching for noteworthy trends — such as an uptick in product sales following a marketing campaign. It looks for correlations, or links between disparate data points, to get to the root of what drives business outcomes. ChatGPT also identifies patterns within text, reading between the lines of qualitative data to gauge public sentiment or catch emerging market trends, much like an economist might analyze market reports.

From this analysis, ChatGPT can unearth a spectrum of insights, from the operational, like which product lines are underperforming, to the strategic, such as where market opportunities may lie. It offers the foresight that could suggest an inventory adjustment before a shortage occurs or recommend a new customer service strategy that aligns with evolving customer needs.

The insights gleaned are as varied as the data it dissects. But the power of ChatGPT lies in its ability to bring forth these insights rapidly and precisely.

By walking through this complex process, one realizes that ChatGPT does not just churn out data; it crafts a narrative that aids in the understanding of a business's inner workings and its place in the market, guiding decisions with the clarity of hard evidence.

ChatGPT analyzes data through advanced machine learning algorithms that are essentially sets of instructions computers use to identify patterns and make predictions. Among these are algorithms for regression, classification, and natural language processing (NLP). Here's how these work in a more detailed breakdown:

For quantitative data, regression algorithms help predict numerical outcomes based on historical data points. If a business tracks historical sales data, the following pseudo code outlines a simple linear regression model, designed to predict future sales based on a single variable, such as advertising spend:

```python
python
# Pseudo code for a simple linear regression model
def linear_regression(data, variable):
    # Summarize the dataset
    mean_data, mean_variable = mean(data), mean(variable)
    variance = sum([(variable[i] - mean_variable) ** 2 for i in range(len(data))])
    covariance = sum([(data[i] - mean_data) * (variable[i] - mean_variable) for i in range(len(data))])


    # Calculate coefficients
    beta = covariance / variance
    alpha = mean_data - beta * mean_variable

    # Return the linear regression function
    return lambda x: alpha + beta * x
```

The `linear_regression` function computes coefficients based on the variance and covariance from the data. The returned function can then predict future sales (`y`) given new advertising spend (`x`).

For qualitative data, NLP algorithms assist in interpreting text. A common task is sentiment analysis, where the machine determines whether the text is positive, negative, or neutral. Here's a pseudo code for a simple sentiment analysis model using the bag-of-words approach:

```python
# Pseudo code for a simple sentiment analysis model
def sentiment_analysis(text, positive_words, negative_words):
    # Tokenize text and create a word frequency dictionary
    word_freq = tokenize_and_count_words(text)

    # Calculate sentiment score
    sentiment_score = 0
    for word in word_freq:
        if word in positive_words:
            sentiment_score += word_freq[word]
        elif word in negative_words:
            sentiment_score -= word_freq[word]


    # Determine sentiment
    if sentiment_score > 0:
        return "Positive"
    elif sentiment_score < 0:
        return "Negative"
    else:
        return "Neutral"
```

In the model above, `tokenize_and_count_words` is a hypothetical function that breaks the text into words and counts them. The sentiment is scored by summing the frequencies of positive and negative words.

In a business context, such algorithms provide the computational power to sift through customer feedback, bringing forth predominant sentiments which can inform product development or marketing strategies. By automating the pattern identification process using these machine learning models, ChatGPT enables businesses to quickly adjust to market dynamics, allocate resources effectively, and tailor offerings to meet consumer expectations.

The transition from raw data to actionable insights involves collecting and preprocessing data, selecting appropriate algorithms, training the models on the data, and finally interpreting the results to inform business decisions. This careful methodology ensures that insights are not only precise and tailored to the business context but are also scalable and repeatable, offering businesses the foresight and adaptability that is essential in the constantly evolving marketplace.

AI-driven data analysis is like equipping decision-makers with a high-powered telescope, allowing them to see far beyond the horizon of traditional data interpretation. The process begins by aggregating diverse data sets, where AI meticulously cleans and sorts through the information, removing noise and identifying relevant points—much like a curator selectively choosing exhibits for a museum display. These refined data sets can include past sales figures, consumer behavior metrics, or even social media commentary—all serving as inputs for the AI's sophisticated algorithms.

With the data in place, AI starts its detective work. It applies statistical models and machine learning techniques that find patterns and relationships within the data. For instance, it could highlight the link between customer support response times and client satisfaction scores, or predict the demand for a product based on seasonal trends. This stage is the equivalent of a mathematician solving complex equations to reveal undiscovered truths.

The output of this analysis, the insight, is what fuels informed decisions. It arrives not as a mere collection of numbers or graphs, but as a clear signpost pointing towards strategic pathways—a forecast of potential outcomes that enables businesses to make preemptive moves rather than reactive ones. A company might use these AI-derived insights to optimize inventory levels ahead of an anticipated busy period, to tailor marketing efforts where they're likely to have the greatest impact or to develop new products that align with emerging consumer needs.

However, it's critical to interpret these insights within the context they're intended for. The AI doesn't make the decisions; it supports the decision-makers. It's a tool that enhances human judgment rather than replaces it, offering a refined lens through which business landscapes can be viewed with greater clarity. This synergy between human intuition and AI analytics represents a new echelon of strategic decision-making, where choices are informed by a depth of data-driven understanding that was once outside our reach. It's not just the future of business—it's the present, an age where companies armed with AI insights operate with the wisdom of forethought and act with decisive precision.

Let's take a detailed exploration into the statistical models and machine learning techniques that AI systems employ to make sense of data. In the context of quantitative data, statistical models like linear and logistic regression serve as workhorses. Linear regression might be used to predict continuous outcomes, such as future sales based on historical data, by drawing a line that best fits the data points. For example, a business might predict next month's sales by analyzing the trend line that plots past sales against time.

Logistic regression, on the other hand, comes into play when the outcome is categorical, like predicting whether an email is spam or not; it places data into discrete buckets. Picture a sorting hat that decides which house each new Hogwarts student belongs to, but in this case, it's an algorithm that categorizes emails based on word patterns.

Machine learning goes a step further by employing algorithms such as decision trees and neural networks. Decision trees sort data through a series of questions, much like a flowchart leading to a conclusion. They might be used to decide if conditions are right for launching a new product, taking into account factors such as market trends and competitor actions. Neural networks, inspired by the human brain, recognize complex patterns through layers of interconnected 'neurons'. These networks can interpret intricate data like consumer behavior to provide recommendations for personalizing marketing campaigns.

When dealing with qualitative data, techniques like sentiment analysis and topic modeling come into play. Sentiment analysis gauges public opinion on a product by categorizing social media posts as positive, negative, or neutral. Imagine a focus group where comments are automatically sorted by the underlying sentiment, giving businesses a gauge of public perception at scale.

Topic modeling, akin to organizing books in a library by subject, picks out the main topics from a collection of texts. A company could use this technique to navigate through thousands of customer reviews and identify common themes and areas of concern.

By harnessing these statistical models and machine learning techniques, AI provides businesses with a toolkit to decode the complexity of data and draw insights that drive strategic action. Machine learning's insights are the compass that guides the ship of a business through the sea of market challenges and opportunities. The clarity these tools offer turns once perplexing data sets into maps that businesses can confidently follow towards sound decisions and, ultimately, success.

Imagine a chef in a bustling kitchen, deftly choosing ingredients from a vast pantry to whip up a culinary masterpiece. In a similar vein, industry titans like Google and Amazon masterfully select from their colossal 'pantries' of data to cook up the next innovation. Their abilities to stay ahead stem from treating data like a versatile ingredient that can create an array of dishes to satisfy any customer's taste.

Google, for instance, akin to a meteorologist predicting weather, uses complex algorithms to forecast digital trends. By analyzing how we interact online, they anticipate our needs, serving up search results or video recommendations with an almost magical foresight. It's a dance between user and provider, where every click and query fine-tunes the rhythm.

Amazon, operating much like a world-class logistician, keeps its operations running as efficiently as a symphony orchestra. It interprets customer data—our shopping habits, preferences, and even the time we linger on a product—to ensure inventory is precisely where it needs to be, just as a conductor ensures each musician is ready to play their part.

These industry leaders don't just use data; they orchestrate it. Their algorithms are the batons guiding the flow of information, turning chaotic streams of data points into harmonious insights that power innovation and efficiency. The choices these giants make, driven by deep dives into massive datasets, are less about intuition and more about the finely-tuned analytics that keep them at the top of their game. It's a world where data isn't just a resource; it's the pulse of an ongoing commitment to meet the future head-on, solidifying their roles as the visionaries of the digital age.

Here is the detailed breakdown of the algorithms and data processing techniques that powerhouses like Google and Amazon employ to stay at the forefront of their industries:

- **Predictive Analytics**
  - **Machine Learning Models**: Use of various models such as linear regression for sales forecasting, logistic regression for customer churn prediction, and time-series analysis for trend forecasting.

- **Big Data Processing**
  - **MapReduce**: A framework that processes large data sets over clusters by mapping a function over the data and then reducing the results.
  - **Data Lakes**: Storage repositories that hold vast amounts of raw data in its native format until needed.

- **Natural Language Processing (NLP)**
  - **Sentiment Analysis**: Algorithms that understand sentiment in customer feedback or reviews by classifying it as positive, negative, or neutral.
  - **Text Classification**: Automated categorizing of text into predefined tags or categories.

- **Search Algorithms**
  - **PageRank**: Used by Google to rank web pages in their search engine based on the quality and quantity of links to the pages.
  - **AutoML**: An end-to-end solution for building custom machine learning models for ranking, categorization, and more without extensive machine learning expertise.

- **Recommendation Systems**
  - **Collaborative Filtering**: Recommending products to users based on the preferences of similar users.
  - **Content-Based Filtering**: Recommendations based on analyzing product details and matching them with user preferences.

- **Operational Optimization**
  - **Supply Chain Optimization**: Integration of complex algorithms for demand forecasting, inventory management, and delivery logistics.
  - **Dynamic Pricing Models**: Utilizing real-time data to adjust prices based on market demand, competition, and inventory levels.

These techniques allow companies to comb through mountains of data, identify meaningful relationships, and make educated predictions for future trends. Unlike rigid, rule-based systems, these algorithms can adapt to new data, improving their predictions over time. Google's and Amazon's prowess in optimizing these algorithms allows them to not only understand current consumer behavior but also to anticipate future changes, often before the consumers themselves do. This strategic prognosis leads to smarter business decisions that are data-backed, ranging from introducing new product lines to optimizing marketing campaigns and improving customer service. The ability of these companies to harness such technology underpins their sustained innovation and operational efficiency.

To integrate ChatGPT within a business, begin with a thorough needs assessment, determining where AI can solve problems or enhance productivity, akin to identifying the right tool for a job. Once the areas are pinpointed, the following phases outline the strategic incorporation of ChatGPT:

- **Initial Planning**: Lay a blueprint where ChatGPT comes into play. Determine whether it will be assisting with customer service, streamlining data analysis, or automating content creation. This phase is like sketching out a mind map with ChatGPT at the center and lines connecting to different business functions.

- **Data Preparation**: Collect and organize the requisite data essential for training ChatGPT. Just as one might compile ingredients before cooking a meal, assemble all relevant information so that ChatGPT can understand the context of the operations.

- **Integration and Deployment**: Plug ChatGPT into the existing business ecosystem, which might involve setting it up as a chatbot on the company website or as a tool within the customer support desk. Here, it's key to ensure smooth interaction with current processes, as if seamlessly adding a new appliance to an electrical grid without overloading it.

- **Training and Customization**: Tailor ChatGPT to meet specific business needs by feeding it industry-specific knowledge and company information. This is analogous to programming a universal remote to control a specific set of devices—it should align with its designated role effortlessly.

- **Testing**: Before going live, simulate real-world scenarios to test ChatGPT's responses and functionality. Consider this the dress rehearsal before the opening night, making sure each line is delivered to perfection.

- **Implementation**: Launch ChatGPT's services to your team and customers. Like unveiling a new product, this introduces a novel dimension to the business's workflow and customer interaction.

- **Monitoring and Feedback**: Continuously observe ChatGPT's performance, gathering feedback from users and making adjustments. It's a process of refinement, similar to editing a draft based on reader critiques to enhance the final copy.

- **Evolution and Scaling**: As ChatGPT learns and improves, scale its usage across different domains of the business, ensuring it grows and adapts with the company's evolution.

By methodically guiding ChatGPT through these stages, businesses can capture its full potential, leading to improved efficiency and innovation. However, it is important to navigate the transition with care, remaining aware of limitations like data sensitivity and the need for human oversight. Successful incorporation means that ChatGPT not only complements but also elevates the business's capabilities, emerging as a reliable and insightful asset in the business's ongoing story of growth and adaptation.

Let's take a deeper look at the crucial phase of 'Monitoring and Feedback' during the integration of ChatGPT into business operations. This is where the effectiveness of the AI is put to the test, and the insights gathered can lead to significant enhancements to the model.

To track performance, we set up clear, quantifiable metrics, such as response accuracy rate, which gauges the percentage of ChatGPT's responses that are correct and relevant to user inquiries. Think of it like a school exam, where each response is a question that ChatGPT must answer accurately to score well.

Another essential metric is the response time, measuring the speed at which ChatGPT provides answers. It's similar to timing a sprinter—businesses aim for gold-medal speeds to ensure customer queries are handled swiftly.

User satisfaction can be evaluated through direct methods like surveys, where users rate their interaction with ChatGPT, or indirectly through analysis of follow-up actions, like whether a user needed additional support after interacting with the AI. Imagine customers filling out a comment card after a dining experience; their feedback is invaluable to the restaurant's improvement.

To iterate the AI model for continuous improvement, businesses look at the gathered metrics and identify trends. For example, if accuracy dips at certain times of the day, perhaps due to high traffic, it indicates a need for adjustment in resource allocation—akin to adding more staff during a restaurant's rush hour for optimal service.

Furthermore, direct user feedback can be used to refine ChatGPT's training data. If users frequently ask questions that ChatGPT cannot answer, this missing information can be incorporated into subsequent training cycles, much like a chef who revises a recipe after patrons suggest an extra pinch of salt.

The 'Monitoring and Feedback' phase is a loop of evaluation and enhancement, ensuring that ChatGPT doesn't just maintain its performance but grows more sophisticated over time. By carefully analyzing data and user interactions, businesses can enable their AI model to evolve, providing continuously improved service that meets consumer needs and expectations while keeping their AI deployment adaptive and robust.

Navigating data analysis often involves tackling obstacles such as incomplete data sets, a reality akin to a puzzle with missing pieces. When pieces are missing, the picture is unclear, just as gaps in data can lead to flawed insights. Tools like ChatGPT assist by extrapolating from existing data to infer the missing pieces, infusing a more complete picture with predictive modeling.

Data cleansing is another routine yet critical hurdle, much like preparing raw ingredients before cooking. It involves scrubbing the data clean of errors, duplicates, or irrelevant information. ChatGPT can automate aspects of this, flagging anomalies and inconsistencies as a spellchecker would in a document, ensuring the dataset's quality and reliability.

Structuring data for AI use can be complex, too. Just as books are organized in a library for easy retrieval, data must be formatted and organized systematically to train AI effectively. With ChatGPT, unstructured data such as free-form text can be sorted and labeled, transforming a jumble of information into a well-ordered database ready for analysis.

Tackling these common challenges requires meticulous attention to detail. Integrating ChatGPT into this process enhances efficiency and accuracy, helping to ensure data is complete, clean, and precisely formulated. By utilizing such AI tools, analysts can focus on drawing deep, actionable insights rather than getting entangled in data preparatory tasks. It's a partnership where ChatGPT's capabilities dovetail with human analytical prowess to pave the way for well-informed decision-making based on data that one can trust. This approach does not only solve immediate issues but also lays the groundwork for a robust data analysis framework that stands the test of time and evolving business needs.

To program ChatGPT or similar AI tools to identify and handle incomplete datasets, one begins by preparing the algorithm to detect gaps. The following step-by-step guide outlines this process:

1. **Identify Missing Values**:
   - The first task is to scan the dataset for missing entries. Pseudo code for this might look like:

```python
python
def find_missing_data(data):
    missing_data_indices = []
    for index, value in enumerate(data):
        if value is None or value == "":
            missing_data_indices.append(index)
    return missing_data_indices
```

2. **Data Imputation**:
   - Strategize how to fill missing values, whether by average, median, or mode for numerical data, or a common string for categorical data. An example of pseudo code for this is:

```python
def impute_missing_data(data, missing_indices, strategy="mean"):
    if strategy == "mean":
        replacement_value = mean([value for index, value in enumerate(data) if index not in missing_indices])
        # ... other strategies like median, mode, etc.

    for index in missing_indices:
        data[index] = replacement_value
    return data
```

3. **Update AI Training**:
   - Incorporate the cleaned data into the model's training cycle, enabling it to learn from a complete picture.

For automating data cleansing, a method might involve the following:

1. **Error Detection**:
   - Create rules and statistical tests to flag anomalies. For instance, if a value in a 'temperature' column exceeds what is physically possible, it should be marked as an outlier.

2. **Anomaly Correction**:
   - Upon detecting these errors, determine whether to correct them using nearest acceptable values, or remove them altogether if they're too severe. Pseudo code could resemble:

```python
def correct_anomalies(data, threshold):
    for index, value in enumerate(data):
        if not (0 <= value <= threshold):  # Assuming threshold is the max valid value
            data[index] = calculate_nearest_acceptable_value(value,
```

threshold)
    return data

3. **Automation**:
- Embed these detection and correction methods into data ingestion pipelines so that ChatGPT processes and cleans data in real-time, ensuring a continuous flow of quality data.

By following these procedures methodically, businesses can lay a foundation for ChatGPT to generate insights from robust, reliable data. This ensures that decision-making is based on the clearest picture possible, with the AI tool smartly predicting and addressing data gaps and ensuring data integrity before it's put to use. It's a proactive approach, maintaining vigilance over data quality, much like a gatekeeper ensuring that only the best-quality ingredients are used in a kitchen, resulting in dependable, insightful output that can be trusted for making critical business decisions.

To construct ChatGPT prompts that yield actionable insights, the process starts with pinpointing the precise information needed. Begin by stating the objective clearly, akin to setting a destination in a GPS. A well-defined goal might be, "Identify the factors leading to increased website traffic." Next, the prompt should be tailored to include relevant specifics, such as, "Compare website traffic from marketing campaigns X, Y, and Z over the last quarter."

Break it down further by requesting data interpretation: "Analyze the correlation between email campaign click-through rates and sales numbers for product A in the first quarter." Here, ChatGPT acts as a focused analyst, delving into the data relationships you've highlighted.

Consider also the timing and granularity of data: "What are the daily peak usage times for our service over the past month?" By specifying the 'when' and the 'how detailed,' ChatGPT's response can shed light on patterns that inform decisions like staffing or feature deployment.

Once the data angle is set, ask for recommendations based on the analysis, for example, "Based on the sales trend from the past month, suggest inventory adjustments for the next cycle." Here, the prompt seeks not just information but strategic advice, leveraging ChatGPT's capacity to simulate decision-making processes.

Finally, validate the insights by requesting data-backed justification: "Explain the rationale behind the inventory adjustment recommendations." This ensures that the strategies are built on solid ground and are not just data outputs but reasoned conclusions.

Each prompt guides ChatGPT through a logical progression of data digestion, analysis, and insight generation, allowing businesses to transform raw figures into strategic steps. It's like transforming a list of raw ingredients into a recipe; with each added detail, the path from data to action becomes clearer, leading to decisions that aren't just reactive but are informed, strategic, and aimed at fostering growth and efficiency.

Here are some ChatGPT prompts designed to extract actionable insights from business data:

- **Sales Driver Analysis** - **Objective**: To identify factors contributing to sales increases.
   - **Prompt**: 'What are the main factors that have contributed to the increase in sales for the last two quarters?'
   - **Sample Output**: 'The main factors contributing to sales increase include a 20% rise in online ad impressions, a 15% increase in repeat customer purchases, and a noticeable uptick in sales during promotional events.'
   - **Follow Up**: Assess the scalability of the contributing factors and devise strategies to amplify these sales drivers further.

- **Campaign Performance Review** - **Objective**: To determine the most successful marketing campaign.
   - **Prompt**: 'Compare the ROI of marketing campaigns A, B, and C over the last financial year.'
   - **Sample Output**: 'Campaign A yielded a 50% ROI, B resulted in 35%, while C achieved 25%. Therefore, campaign A had the most substantial impact on financial returns.'
   - **Follow Up**: Analyze the components of Campaign A to understand why it outperformed others and apply these insights to future campaigns.

- **Customer Satisfaction Insight** - **Objective**: To gauge customer feedback for product improvement.

130

- **Prompt**: 'Analyze customer reviews for product X in the last six months; summarize common praises and complaints.'
- **Sample Output**: 'Customers frequently praised product X for its durability and user-friendly design but commonly cited limited color options as a drawback.'
- **Follow Up**: Consider incorporating the feedback into product design where feasible and communicate potential changes to customers.

- **Efficiency Optimization** - **Objective**: To pinpoint operational inefficiencies in the workflow.
- **Prompt**: 'Identify any bottlenecks in the current manufacturing process that may hinder productivity.'
- **Sample Output**: 'The most significant bottleneck is at the assembly stage, where a lack of automated processes results in a 20% longer production time compared to industry standards.'
- **Follow Up**: Explore options for process automation and consider implementing technology to streamline workflow.

- **Inventory Adjustment Strategy** - **Objective**: To optimize inventory levels based on demand projections.
- **Prompt**: 'Predict inventory requirements for the next quarter based on previous sales trends and upcoming seasonal demand cycles.'
- **Sample Output**: 'Considering past sales and seasonal spikes, recommend a 30% inventory increase for the high-demand period to prevent stockouts.'
- **Follow Up**: Adjust procurement and storage plans accordingly and monitor sales closely to ensure the forecast aligns with real-time demand.

By executing these ChatGPT prompts, you will gain:

- A clear understanding of key performance indicators for your business, such as sales growth factors.
- Insights into the success of different marketing campaigns by analyzing their return on investment.
- Direct feedback from customers which can inform product improvements and innovation.
- Knowledge of any operational inefficiencies in your processes that could be hindering productivity.
- Data-informed strategies for inventory management, reducing the risk of stockouts or excess supply during demand fluctuations.

In the landscape of strategic business decision-making, ChatGPT can be a powerful ally, providing tailored responses based on complex data analysis. For example, a business professional contemplating market expansion might use the prompt, "Assess the potential market size and growth for product X in region Y over the next five years." This would yield projections to inform whether an expansion could be lucrative.

Another prompt might be, "Given historical data on sales and marketing spend, what is the expected return on investment if we increase our marketing budget by 20%?" ChatGPT would analyze past trends and spending efficacy to predict future returns, guiding budget allocation decisions.

Consider a company facing supply chain disruptions; the prompt could be, "Model the impact of a 10% increase in raw material costs on our end product's price and profit margins." Here, ChatGPT would apply financial modeling to provide a detailed impact analysis, aiding in price adjustment strategies.

Each prompt steers ChatGPT to dissect and synthesize data into strategic insights, much like a navigator plotting a course through a complex landscape. These insights enable professionals to move forward, not on hunches, but on informed predictions that chart a path to business objectives. The crux of utilizing such prompts lies in their precision and contextual alignment with the business's unique challenges and data environment.

Here are some ChatGPT prompts that revolve around strategic business decision-making:

Market Size Estimation - **Objective**: Project market size and growth for strategic planning.
- **Prompt**: 'Estimate the market size and growth rate for electric vehicles in the Midwest region over the next five years.'
- **Sample Output**: 'The market size for electric vehicles in the Midwest is currently estimated at $2 billion, with a projected annual growth rate of 15% over the next five years.'
- **Follow Up**: Consider whether the company's current capabilities can meet this growing demand or if there's a need to invest in expanding

operations in the Midwest region.

ROI Calculation - **Objective**: Measure the return on increased marketing spend.
- **Prompt**: 'Calculate the return on investment for a 20% increase in the digital marketing budget based on last year's sales data.'
- **Sample Output**: 'Increasing the digital marketing budget by 20% is projected to yield an additional $500,000 in sales, constituting an ROI of 150%.'
- **Follow Up**: Decide if investing in digital marketing aligns with current financial strategies and determine specific areas for budget reallocation.

Impact Modeling - **Objective**: Model the financial impact of increased costs.
- **Prompt**: 'Model the impact on our profit margin if the cost of raw materials increases by 5%, considering our current pricing strategy.'
- **Sample Output**: 'A 5% increase in raw material costs could result in a 2% decrease in profit margins unless prices are adjusted accordingly.'
- **Follow Up**: Evaluate pricing strategies to offset rising costs without losing competitiveness or review the potential to negotiate with suppliers for better rates.

Operational Efficiency - **Objective**: Identify and remedy operational bottlenecks.
- **Prompt**: 'Analyze the production workflow to find bottlenecks that occurred in Q2 and suggest process improvements.'
- **Sample Output**: 'Bottlenecks were identified in the assembly line and quality control, causing delays. Implementing an automated assembly system and additional QA checkpoints is recommended to improve flow.'
- **Follow Up**: Assess the feasibility and cost of implementing the suggested improvements and develop an implementation timeline.

Product Development Strategy - **Objective**: Discover opportunities for innovation.
- **Prompt**: 'Analyze customer feedback on our software products from the last six months to identify features for development.'
- **Sample Output**: 'Customers frequently request an enhancement to the data visualization capabilities of our software. Developing this feature could increase user satisfaction and market competitiveness.'

- **Follow Up**: Task the product development team to create a prototype of the new data visualization feature and conduct market testing.

Customer Retention Analysis - **Objective**: Understand drivers behind customer churn.

- **Prompt**: 'Identify common factors among customers who cancelled their subscriptions in the past three months.'

- **Sample Output**: 'Customers often cited a lack of advanced features and competitive pricing options as reasons for cancellation.'

- **Follow Up**: Explore options to enhance product features and reevaluate pricing structures to better meet customer expectations.

Demand Forecasting - **Objective**: Predict future product demand to inform inventory management.

- **Prompt**: 'Forecast the demand for our new product line in the upcoming quarter using historical sales data from similar product launches.'

- **Sample Output**: 'The demand for the new product line is projected to exceed previous launches by 20%, suggesting a need for increased inventory.'

- **Follow Up**: Adjust procurement and production schedules to ensure sufficient inventory levels are maintained to meet the forecasted demand.

Competitive Analysis - **Objective**: Assess the competitive landscape to develop strategic initiatives.

- **Prompt**: 'Compare our market share and growth rate with our top three competitors in the past year.'

- **Sample Output**: 'Our market share has grown by 8%, while our competitors have shown an average of 5% growth. However, competitor B launched a new product feature that is gaining traction.'

- **Follow Up**: Analyze competitor B's new feature and determine if a similar innovation or an alternative competitive strategy is needed.

Marketing Strategy Optimization - **Objective**: Optimize marketing strategies for higher engagement.

- **Prompt**: 'What are the performance metrics of our latest marketing campaign, and how do they correlate with increased user engagement?'

- **Sample Output**: 'The campaign resulted in a 30% rise in social media interactions and a 10% increase in website traffic, which correlates with a higher user engagement on the platform.'

- **Follow Up**: Capitalize on the successful tactics of the latest campaign and consider increasing focus on the most responsive marketing channels.

Risk Assessment - **Objective**: Evaluate potential risks involved with a new business venture.

- **Prompt**: 'Conduct a risk analysis for entering the healthcare tech market by next year.'

- **Sample Output**: 'Potential risks include regulatory hurdles, significant capital investment required upfront, and strong competition from existing healthcare tech companies.'

- **Follow Up**: Weigh the identified risks against potential rewards, and if proceeding, develop a detailed risk mitigation plan.

By executing these prompts, you will tap into a methodical analysis of various strategic facets of your business operations. You gain a nuanced understanding of customer retention by pinpointing why customers may be leaving, allowing you to address these issues directly. Through demand forecasting, you're gifted foresight, like a captain reading the stars, to navigate inventory management proactively.

Competitive analysis furnishes you with a bird's-eye view of your market positioning, compared to your rivals, empowering you to make tactical decisions. Delving into the analysis of your marketing strategy shines a spotlight on what really resonates with your audience, helping to tailor future campaigns for maximum engagement. Lastly, risk assessment equips you with the knowledge to either brace for potential storms or chart a new course away from troubled waters if contemplating a venture into new markets. Each executed prompt isn't just a task completed; it's actionable intelligence accrued—a beacon to illuminate the path toward strategic growth and stability.

In sum, by executing all the prompts, we:

- Gained clarity on the underlying reasons for customer churn to improve retention strategies.
- Anticipated product demand to align inventory with future sales, avoiding overstocking or stockouts.
- Compared our market performance against competitors, identifying areas for strategic improvement.
- Analyzed the impact of marketing strategies on customer engagement to optimize future campaigns.
- Evaluated the risk landscape of a potential new business venture to make informed strategic decisions.

When crafting ChatGPT prompts with an eye towards shaping holistic business strategies, it's akin to casting a wide net in the open sea of data, aiming to capture a diverse catch of insights. One would use a prompt like, "What patterns can be observed from our year-over-year growth data that suggest a pivot in our business model?" It's asking for a macroscopic analysis that might highlight pivotal trends requiring strategic action, such as diversifying product lines. Another such prompt may be, "Assess how consumer behavior has shifted in our industry in the last decade and the implications for our long-term strategic goals." This type of inquiry leans on the AI's ability to cross-reference and contextualize vast swaths of consumer data, compiling a narrative that frames the future direction of an industry.

Each of these expansive prompts is a request for ChatGPT to comb through the strands of collected data and weave them into a cohesive whole, one that reveals not just disparate facts but a storyline of past, present, and potential future. Outcomes from these prompts do more than answer questions; they serve as guiding lights for high-level decision-making, providing a compass for navigating the broader operational and competitive landscape. By using ChatGPT in this strategic capacity, a business equips itself with a virtual think tank, capable of elucidating the subtle interplays of market dynamics that inform successful, forward-looking strategies.

Here are some Metaprompts that revolve around strategic business strategy formulation using ChatGPT:

Trend Analysis for Strategic Development - **Objective**: To create prompts that identify key trends affecting business growth and development.
- **ChatGPT MetaPrompt**: 'Generate a list of prompts that analyze significant trends from our business's historical data and suggest areas for strategic innovation or redirection.'
- **Expected Output**: Prompts that lead to trend analysis in sales, customer behavior, market shifts, and technology adoption, which can drive strategic business decisions.
- **Follow Up**: Use the resulting prompts to conduct an in-depth trend analysis and align the findings with business strategy planning sessions.

Consumer Behavior Insight Mining - **Objective**: To formulate prompts that uncover changes in consumer behavior and the impact on the business.

- **ChatGPT MetaPrompt**: 'Devise prompts that assess the evolution of customer preferences and purchasing behaviors over the last ten years in our industry.'
- **Expected Output**: A set of prompts aimed at revealing how consumer behavior has shifted, helping to guide product development, marketing, and customer experience strategies.
- **Follow Up**: Implement the discoveries of these consumer behavior analyses into strategic planning for product and service offerings.

Competitive Landscape Navigation - **Objective**: To produce prompts that explore the competitive environment and suggest adaptive strategies.
- **ChatGPT MetaPrompt**: 'Craft a comprehensive list of prompts to explore our current competitive standing in the market and potential strategies to strengthen our position.'
- **Expected Output**: Prompts focused on evaluating competitive threats, opportunities, and strategies that relate to the company's market positioning.
- **Follow Up**: Analyze the strategic insights and incorporate them into business development strategies and competitive positioning tactics.

Innovation Opportunities Identification - **Objective**: To generate prompts that seek out innovation opportunities within the market data.
- **ChatGPT MetaPrompt**: 'Create prompts that guide us toward uncovering gaps in the market that our company could innovatively fill.'
- **Expected Output**: A series of prompts that help identify unmet customer needs or emerging technology trends to capitalize on for innovation.
- **Follow Up**: Collate the responses to shape an innovation pipeline and guide research and development investments.

Operational Efficiency Improvement - **Objective**: To establish prompts that help pinpoint operational inefficiencies.
- **ChatGPT MetaPrompt**: 'Develop a set of prompts for investigating inefficient areas of our operations and proposing data-driven solutions to optimize them.'
- **Expected Output**: Prompts that dig into operational workflows, identifying bottlenecks and suggesting procedural or technological enhancements.
- **Follow Up**: Take the operational insights and assess the feasibility of implementing the solutions, looking towards improving efficiency and reducing costs.

By executing these metaprompts, you will gain:

- A roadmap that guides you through the discovery of key trends that can reshape your business strategy, much like finding signposts that point toward new paths to success.
- Insights into how consumer behaviors have evolved, enabling you to adjust your offerings and communications in ways that resonate with today's market.
- A deeper understanding of your competitive landscape, providing the clarity needed to forge strategies that can help you stand out in a crowded marketplace.
- Inspiration for innovation by identifying gaps in the market, leading to opportunities that could set your company apart from the competition.
- Strategies to optimize your operations by pinpointing inefficiencies, which could save time and resources and enhance your company's overall effectiveness.

Imagine you're a detective in a mystery novel. In this story, data analysis is your magnifying glass, allowing you to uncover clues and patterns that are not apparent at first glance. Advanced data analysis methods are like different detective tools in your kit—they might look intimidating, but each has a particular strength that helps crack the case.

For example, machine learning is like a trusty sidekick who learns by your side. You show them examples of past solved cases (or data), and they pick up on the patterns, such as "all suspects wearing green hats were innocent." With enough training, the sidekick can start making educated guesses about new mysteries based on those patterns.

Data mining is your process of sifting through the sand to find hidden gems. Imagine you're at the beach with a metal detector, waving it back and forth over the sand. Every beep is a potential clue. In the business world, this detector is sifting through rows of data looking for anomalies, trends, or specific information that can lead to a breakthrough insight.

The workflow is your detective story's plot. It starts with a question or a problem, follows through the investigation of data (collecting clues), moves on to analysis (piecing together the evidence) and ends with conclusions (solving the mystery). Each chapter is important because it builds on the previous one, leading to that moment of revelation.

By understanding these concepts as parts of a detective story, data analysis becomes a thrilling adventure. You realize it's not just about numbers on a screen; it's a quest for truth, powered by logic, patterns, and yes, a bit of intuition. And just like any good detective story, there's always more to learn, more tools to add to your toolbox, and more cases to crack.

Here is the breakdown of the machine learning workflow, unraveling each stage as if following a recipe to bake a delicious cake:

- **Data Collection**
- Gathering ingredients: Just as you need the right ingredients to start baking, you begin by collecting the data you need for your machine learning project.
- Sources: This can come from various places, like customer surveys, sensors, online behavior, or sales records.

- **Data Cleaning**
- Preparing your ingredients: Before you bake, you need to make sure your ingredients are clean and ready to use. You do the same with your data, removing anything that's irrelevant, correcting errors, or filling in missing pieces.

- **Data Exploration**
- Understanding the flavors: A chef needs to taste and understand their ingredients; similarly, you explore the data to find patterns or interesting facts that could help with your machine learning.
- Visualization: Like laying out your ingredients before you start, visualizing data can help you see what you're working with, using graphs or charts.

- **Feature Selection**
- Choosing the right flavors: Not every ingredient is needed for a cake. You choose the most important features (aspects of the data) that will help your machine learning model learn effectively.

- Model Training
- Mixing and baking: This is where you mix your ingredients following your recipe (algorithm) and bake your cake (train your model). The machine learning model tries to learn from the data it's given, as if you're teaching it a family recipe.

- Model Evaluation
- Taste testing: Just as you'd taste a cake to see if it needs more flavor, you evaluate your machine learning model to see how well it has learned. If it's not doing a good job, like a bland cake, you might need to go back and adjust your recipe (algorithm) or get better quality ingredients (data).

- Model Tuning
- Perfecting your recipe: If your cake isn't fluffy enough, you tweak your recipe. Similarly, you adjust your machine learning model - maybe by picking better features or tuning the algorithm settings - until it performs just right.

- Model Deployment
- Serving the cake: Once you're happy with your cake, you serve it. With a machine learning model, you deploy it so that it can start making predictions or decisions based on new data it hasn't seen before, just like guests trying your cake.

- Monitoring and Maintenance
- Keeping the cake fresh: A cake can go stale, and so can a machine learning model. You keep an eye on it and update it with fresh data, ensuring it keeps performing well over time.

By understanding each of these stages and their function, it becomes less like a mysterious high-tech procedure and more like a series of intentional, understandable steps towards creating something valuable, whether it's a delightful cake or a smart, learning machine.

Mastering data analysis with ChatGPT equips business professionals with a powerful tool for navigating the wealth of information that modern businesses generate. With ChatGPT, the complex becomes accessible, as it processes and interprets vast datasets, discerning trends, patterns, and anomalies that could escape the human eye. This ability enables professionals to sift through noise and focus on what matters, turning data into actionable knowledge that underpins informed and strategic decision-making.

Armed with these insights, business leaders can approach choices not only with confidence but with a clarity that is rooted in data-driven analysis. The strategic edge gained from ChatGPT's sophisticated analysis allows for decisions that are timely, relevant, and tailored to the unique challenges and opportunities each business faces. In sum, mastering data analysis with ChatGPT is not simply about responding to the data at hand; it's about shaping a strategy that positions the enterprise to thrive in an ever-evolving marketplace.

SCALING YOUR BUSINESS AND FUTURE PLANNING

Scaling a business is akin to nurturing a plant. Just as a gardener must provide the right conditions for growth—nutrient-rich soil, water, and sunlight—so must a business create an environment where it can flourish. This chapter lays out the fundamental soil of knowledge needed to nourish a business's roots, the strategies that let it branch out confidently, and the insights acting as sunlight to spur continued growth.

These strategies aren't just theoretical; they're proven through practice and are as critical to business success as water is to life. Understanding the dynamics of customer demand, the flow of market trends, and the efficiency of operational processes will shape the trajectory of a company's expansion. It's about ensuring that growth is not only achievable, but sustainable and resilient—like a tree that stands tall through the seasons. This chapter is about equipping readers to cultivate their business landscape with the skill of an experienced gardener, anticipating and responding to change with wisdom and foresight. Each concept is unpicked and laid out in a logical progression, building upon one another to form a cohesive guide for growth.

Business scalability is the ability of a company to sustain or improve its performance when its sales volume increases. Think of it like a busy coffee shop. If a small shop can serve 50 customers a day efficiently, but starts to struggle with 100, it's not scalable. A scalable business would handle that increase without compromising service quality or increasing costs proportionally.

Scalability involves smart planning and the strategic use of resources. It requires systems that can adapt to larger demands—like a kitchen that can serve either a small family or a large party with the same level of quality. It's about having flexible processes that can expand and contract without breaking. You need technology that scales; a website that runs just as smoothly with 1,000 visitors as it does with 100. You have to build a team that grows with the business, where the addition of new members is like adding blocks to a tower without it toppling over.

The significance of scalability lies in its ability to multiply revenue with minimal incremental cost. A scalable business can take on more work with less stress on its systems and structures. Done right, it's the difference between a business that thrives under pressure and one that buckles. Like a well-designed bridge that can bear the weight of heavy traffic, scalability ensures your business can handle growth and thrive under the weight of success.

Let's take a deeper look at the nuts and bolts of crafting scalable systems in a business. These systems are the backbone that supports growth, much like how a sturdy frame is essential for a building to withstand the addition of more floors.

Firstly, technology must be at the heart of scalable systems. Consider your business's technological infrastructure like the plumbing and electrical work in a high-rise building: it needs to handle increased capacity without faltering. This means investing in cloud-based software that can grow with your user base or customer demands, ensuring that your online storefront remains seamless, whether it's handling a hundred or a million transactions.

Next are personnel and team structures. Expanding a business without carefully thought-out team dynamics is like adding more players to a sports team without a plan: it can lead to chaos. Structuring your teams with clear roles and responsibilities, while maintaining fluid communication channels, ensures that as new hires are onboarded, everyone knows their position and how to interact effectively, maintaining the agility that smaller companies enjoy.

As for operations, we are talking about the day-to-day business processes that keep the gears turning. To make these processes scalable, they must be standardized and documented. This is much like creating a manual for assembling a complex piece of machinery—with the right instructions, anyone can step in and put it together. Ensuring that operational processes are repeatable and efficient means that increasing workloads won't lead to breakdowns in production or service delivery.

By taking the time to install these scalable systems thoughtfully, businesses are not just preparing to grow; they are equipping themselves to manage that growth successfully. The goal is a flexible and robust framework that can support both current operations and future expansion—creating a business that not only grows but scales smart.

Using data for strategic business expansion is like planning a big road trip. Before you set off, you gather information about possible routes, check weather forecasts, and consider past trips to predict traffic conditions. This preparation, your data collection, helps you decide the best way to go, when to leave, and what you might encounter along the way.

The data analysis itself is akin to looking at a map with various highlighted paths. Just as you'd weigh the benefits of a scenic route against a faster highway, a company examines trends, customer behaviors, and sales patterns to chart the course for growth. It's about making choices that save time and fuel, maximizing efficiency and enjoyment.

Then, with the trip underway, imagine the ongoing adjustments you make based on real-time GPS updates. This is like responsive data analysis, allowing a business to shift strategies when sales take an unexpected turn, or a new competitor enters the market—think of it as rerouting due to an unforeseen roadblock or traffic jam.

Understanding data for strategic expansion is about seeing it as the compass, map, and GPS system that guides a business on its growth journey—identifying the most promising roads to take, foreseeing potential detours, and navigating the route to success.

Here is the breakdown of the data analysis process for business expansion, laid out to enhance understanding and application:

- **Data Collection**
    - Identifying Data Sources:
        - Start by pinpointing where the relevant data lives.
        - This could include sales records, customer feedback, or website traffic statistics.
    - Gathering Data:
        - Use tools or services to collect the data efficiently and accurately.
        - Make sure the collected data is as complete and error-free as possible.

- **Data Cleaning**
- Removing Irrelevant Information:
- Just like sifting out unwanted items from a drawer, discard data that isn't useful for your analysis.
- Correcting Errors:
- Spot and correct inaccuracies—mistyped numbers, duplicated entries, etc.

- **Data Analysis**
- Interpreting Data:
- Look for patterns and trends, which are like puzzle pieces revealing a bigger picture.
- For instance, identify times of the year when sales peak.
- Utilizing Analytical Tools:
- Apply software tools to manipulate and examine the data.

- **Decision Making**
- Assessing Options:
- Evaluate what the interpreted data suggests about business opportunities.
- Decisions could range from introducing a new product line to changing marketing strategies.
- Risk Evaluation:
- Anticipate potential risks in each choice and weigh them against the expected benefits.

- **Action Steps**
- Implementing Decisions:
- Translate decisions into real-world actions, such as reallocating budget or redesigning a product.
- Tracking Results:
- Monitor the outcomes of your actions to see if they align with predictions made by data analysis.
- Adjust your strategy based on what the results indicate.

By breaking down these components in an easy-to-follow format, you, the reader, are empowered not only with a foundational knowledge of data analysis for business expansion but also with the insight to use this knowledge in actionable, result-driven ways.

Accurate forecasting is the compass that guides a business through the unpredictable seas of the market, steering future planning toward prosperous horizons. It's the process of using historical data, current market trends, and educated assumptions to predict future conditions and performance. Just like a weather forecast helps one dress appropriately for the day, accurate business forecasting helps companies prepare effectively for the future.

This foresight is crucial for business scaling because it allows for the anticipation of demand, the allocation of resources, and the strategic timing of market entry. For a business to scale effectively, it must not only meet current customer needs but also anticipate and plan for future opportunities and challenges. Accurate forecasting lights the path for these decisions, like a lighthouse signaling safe passage for ships navigating dangerous waters.

In essence, the better a company can forecast, the better it can plan and execute strategies that support sustained growth and prevent overextension. In failing to do so, a business might find itself ill-equipped for a surge in demand, missing out on potential sales, or overspending on inventory that goes unsold. Clear, detailed, and careful forecasting is, therefore, not a luxury but a linchpin in the architecture of a business's expansion strategy. It is about equipping oneself with the knowledge and methodologies to make informed decisions that mold the future success of one's business foundation.

Creating an accurate forecast for business expansion is akin to planning a large event. Here's a step-by-step guide to understanding and crafting such a forecast:

Step 1: Gather Historical Data
- Collect sales reports, customer feedback, and market analysis from previous years.
- Like gathering guest feedback from past events, this step helps understand what worked and what didn't.

Step 2: Analyze the Historical Data
- Look for patterns in sales peaks, product popularity, or customer engagement.
- It's similar to noticing which dishes were most popular at past events to

plan future menus.

Step 3: Assess Current Market Trends
- Use market research and current industry reports to understand the present landscape.
- Think of this as checking what type of events are trending now to decide on the event's theme.

Step 4: Make Educated Assumptions
- Based on the historical data and current trends, make predictions about future behaviors and possibilities.
- This resembles anticipating how many guests might attend the next event based on previous interest.

Step 5: Model Forecasting Scenarios
- Create different potential outcomes based on varying factors such as economic conditions or new product launches.
- Imagine planning for different event sizes in case fewer or more guests RSVP than expected.

Step 6: Interpret the Forecast Data
- Draw conclusions from the forecasting models to guide decision-making.
- This is deciding how much food to order or how many staff to hire for the event based on the anticipated guest count.

Step 7: Implement Decisions and Allocate Resources
- Use the forecasts to determine where to invest funds and resources for the best chance at expansion.
- Like using the predicted guest count to allocate the budget for venue, catering, and entertainment accordingly.

Each stage directly ties into the last, forming a cohesive strategy for expanding your business. Like planning an event successfully, a thorough and accurate forecast lets you scale your business effectively, with full knowledge of the potential outcomes and confidence in the decisions you make.

Building scalable systems is about creating a framework within a business that can effortlessly expand along with its growth. These systems are the pulleys and levers that allow companies to service ten customers or ten thousand with the same ease. By integrating technologies that automatically adjust to workload, structuring teams that grow without losing efficiency, and implementing processes that can be repeatably executed on a larger scale, a business creates a foundation much like the roots of a tree. Just as roots support a sapling or a giant oak without change, scalable systems are designed to support a business whether it's just starting out or is a massive enterprise.

The process includes leveraging cloud-based technology to accommodate an increasing number of users without degradation in performance, establishing team protocols that remain effective regardless of team size, and standardizing operations to ensure consistency in product or service quality. These measures serve to empower a company to successfully navigate the challenges that come with expansion while maintaining the integrity of its original mission and vision.

In essence, scalable systems are the bedrock of business growth, enabling companies to anticipate and accommodate expansion without succumbing to the stressors of change. As a guide might detail the layout and construction of a fortress designed to last centuries, so does building scalable systems fortify a business for the long haul, ensuring it stands robust against the tests of time and competition.

Innovation and adaptability in the business world are like the tools in a Swiss Army knife—compact but incredibly versatile when addressing a wide array of challenges. Just as one might use the different tools to tweak a loose screw, snip a stray thread, or open a stubborn bottle, a business uses innovation to refine its products, cut unnecessary costs, and unlock new market opportunities. Adaptability is the hand that wields the knife, adjusting the tool selection in response to the problem at hand. Whether facing the complexities of changing market regulations or the simplicity of optimizing internal processes, businesses pivot and adjust with the finesse of a chef altering a recipe to better suit evolving taste preferences.

Just as you'd intuitively reach for a flashlight when the power goes out, businesses instinctively lean into innovative thinking when navigating the murky waters of growth. This mindset illuminates paths that may otherwise remain obscured, guiding companies through the unpredictable terrain of expansion. The integration of innovative practices and an adaptable spirit ensures that a business can not only solve the puzzles of growth but also preemptively prepare for them, crafting solutions that are as effective and nuanced as using the perfect tool for a repair job at home.

Let's take a deeper look at practical ways to embed innovation and adaptability into the fabric of a business. Effective innovation, like lean methodology, is about trimming the fat from processes—identifying inefficiencies and removing them. A business adopting this approach might use continuous feedback loops from all levels, analyzing every step of product development or service delivery to cut waste and focus on value.

Agile project management, on the other hand, introduces flexibility and iterative progress into operations. It's like building with LEGO blocks, allowing teams to construct, assess, and adjust projects rapidly according to changing requirements, rather than sticking rigidly to a blueprint that may be outdated by the time the project is complete.

When it comes to adaptability, diversifying product lines can be akin to a skilled investor's portfolio. Just as a mix of stocks, bonds, and other assets can help weather financial storms, offering a variety of products or services allows a business to stabilize its revenue streams, even if demand for one area dips.

Restructuring for market responsiveness is similar to redecorating a home. Rooms, or departments, are rearranged to better suit the changing needs of the household—or market conditions. This might mean breaking down silos between departments for better communication and collaboration, streamlining decision-making to allow for quicker responses to change.

These innovative and adaptive practices are woven through the daily routine of a business in meetings that solicit candid feedback, in project sprints that deliver workable results in weeks instead of months, and in strategy sessions that look beyond the current market to anticipate shifts on the horizon.

By incorporating such strategies into everyday operations, businesses hone their edge and flexibility, primed to seize opportunities and pivot away from pitfalls. Understanding these practices and integrating them at the core level ensures that a business remains dynamic, proactive, and resilient, no matter the challenge ahead.

In business scaling, identifying and mitigating risks ensures that growth is not a precarious leap but a measured climb towards expansion. Risk identification begins with thorough analysis: surveying the industry landscape for potential market shifts, evaluating internal processes for hidden inefficiencies, and scanning the financial horizon for cost fluctuations. This is akin to checking a vehicle before a road trip for any signs of trouble that could cause a breakdown.

Once identified, quantifying risks puts a scale to potential problems, much like a doctor assesses the severity of an ailment before treatment. This informs how much attention and resources to allocate to each identified risk. The method of mitigation then depends on the nature of the risk—some may require insurance policies, like wearing a seatbelt, while others call for improving operational processes, akin to driver training to prevent accidents.

Mitigation strategies could involve diversifying product lines to buffer against market volatility, similar to an investor spreading holdings across various asset classes. It may also mean ramping up cybersecurity measures as one would install a home security system to shield against potential break-ins. In each case, the business takes steps to protect its growth trajectory, ensuring longevity and stability.

A coherent strategy for risk management in business scaling not only safeguards current operations but also fortifies the infrastructure against future challenges. It acts as both shield and radar, deflecting immediate threats while scanning the horizon for the next potential challenge, allowing a business to grow with confidence and resilience.

Conducting risk identification, quantification, and the development of mitigation strategies in a business scaling context follows a structured, systematic process, akin to preparing for a voyage at sea with a meticulous attention to safety and preparedness.

1. Risk Identification:

- Perform a comprehensive review of all business areas: For each department, from production to human resources, identify anything that could go wrong.

- Conduct market analysis: Regularly analyze the market to anticipate changes that might affect your business, like a new competitor entering the space or shifts in customer preferences.

- Survey historical data: Look at past challenges your business faced and consider if they could happen again, perhaps on a larger scale due to growth.

2. Risk Quantification:

- Assess the likelihood: Determine the probability of each identified risk. This can be similar to a weather forecast predicting the chance of rain.

- Determine potential impact: Evaluate how each risk could affect your business, from minor disruptions to major setbacks.

- Prioritize risks: Rank the risks based on their potential impact and the likelihood of occurrence, focusing resources on the most significant threats.

3. Developing Mitigation Strategies:

- Design responsive plans: For high-priority risks, develop strategies to either prevent the risk or lessen its impact. This might involve creating backup plans or diversifying your product line.

- Implement controls and processes: Put systems in place that will detect risks early on, much like smoke detectors in a building to catch a fire outbreak before it spreads.

- Continuous monitoring: Establish a continual review process to ensure that the risk management strategies remain effective and responsive.

This approach is iterative and proactive, showing businesses not only how to prepare for known challenges but also how to remain agile enough to respond to unforeseen events. By diligently following these steps, a business ensures a safe passage through the complexities of growth, utilizing risk management as both a shield and a guide through uncharted waters.

Strong leadership is the keystone in the arch of business growth; without it, the structure cannot stand. As a business scales, a leader acts as the navigator, setting the course and adjusting the sails as conditions change. This individual or group of individuals must possess a clear vision for the company's direction, a robust understanding of the business landscape, and the ability to make decisive and strategic choices that will propel the company forward.

Every aspect of scaling, from securing funding for expansion to making critical hires and developing new market strategies, relies on the foresight and direction of its leaders. It is their responsibility to keep teams united and focused, culture intact, and operations running smoothly—even as the complexity of the business increases. Just as a captain ensures that all parts of a ship function together harmoniously to reach a destination, strong leaders synchronize all elements of the company toward achieving growth goals.

In communicating the vision and strategies for scaling, leaders must be transparent with their intentions and open to feedback, affording every member a sense of involvement and clarity on the company's trajectory. Good leadership in the scaling process is about anticipating needs, preparing for challenges, and executing plans with precision and adaptability. It's this leadership that transforms ambitious blueprints into realities, guiding businesses into their next chapters of success.

ChatGPT offers a new frontier in business planning, acting much like an intelligent advisor who can analyze vast amounts of information to provide strategic insights. This AI's capability to learn from patterns and make data-driven predictions is instrumental in formulating effective business strategies. To leverage ChatGPT, begin by feeding it with specific information regarding past performance, market research, and competitive analysis. In return, the system can identify trends and outliers that might not be immediately obvious.

Use ChatGPT to simulate different business scenarios by asking it to process hypothetical situations like market changes or new marketing campaigns. This is similar to a chess player thinking several moves ahead, considering various potential outcomes. It allows businesses to plan with a degree of foresight that was previously more challenging to achieve.

Additionally, ChatGPT can optimize resource allocation. By analyzing productivity data and financial reports, it can suggest where to cut costs and where to invest, ensuring that financial resources strengthen the business's strategic areas. It can also keep abreast of industry developments, regulatory changes, and technological advancements, flagging up relevant news and suggesting how it might impact the business.

However, one must remember that AI, including ChatGPT, is a tool. It needs clear instructions and accurate data to provide valuable insights. The responsibility remains with business leaders to interpret these suggestions wisely, integrate them sensibly into their broader strategy, and maintain a human touch in decision-making. By using ChatGPT judiciously, businesses can augment their planning capacities, making strategies that are not only responsive to current data but are adaptive to future possibilities.

Here are some ChatGPT prompts that revolve around leveraging AI for strategic business planning:

Evaluate Historical Sales Performance - **Objective**: Gain insights into sales trends over time to inform strategy.
- **Prompt**: 'Review the attached sales data from the past five years and provide a report identifying any recurring trends, patterns, and anomalies.'
- **Sample Output**: 'The report shows a consistent increase in sales during the Q2 period, with a notable dip in Q4 of the last two years. Product X consistently outperforms others, especially in the 18-24 age demographic.'
- **Follow Up**: Use the insights to adjust production schedules and marketing strategies for the coming year, and investigate further into the cause of Q4 sales dip.

Market Research Analysis - **Objective**: Compare current market conditions with the company's position.
- **Prompt**: 'Analyze the latest market research findings to determine how our product positioning aligns with consumer expectations and demands.'
- **Sample Output**: 'The analysis indicates that while our pricing is competitive, there is a growing demand for features that are currently only offered by our competitors. Adjusting our product features could improve market share.'
- **Follow Up**: Explore cost-effective ways to enhance product features and realign marketing messages to address consumer demands.

Business Scenario Planning - **Objective**: Prepare for potential future market changes.
- **Prompt**: 'Given a 10% industry-wide increase in material costs next quarter, project how our finances and production might be affected.'
- **Sample Output**: 'A 10% increase in material costs could result in a decrease in our overall profit margin by 3%. Suggested measures include

renegotiating supplier contracts or exploring alternative materials.'
- **Follow Up**: Develop a risk management plan to mitigate the financial impact of rising material costs. Consider strategic supplier partnerships or investments in cost-saving technologies.

Resource Optimization Simulation - **Objective**: Optimize the allocation of company resources.
- **Prompt**: 'Simulate the reallocation of resources from underperforming products to promising R&D projects based on the provided data.'
- **Sample Output**: 'Redirecting 15% of resources from product Y to the new R&D initiative could result in a potential 20% revenue increase in the next fiscal year.'
- **Follow Up**: Conduct a detailed cost-benefit analysis of the proposed resource reallocation and prepare a proposal for stakeholder review.

Industry Development Monitoring - **Objective**: Stay updated with industry trends and their implications.
- **Prompt**: 'Create a system to monitor and summarize technological advancements in our sector over the next six months.'
- **Sample Output**: 'The system has identified an emerging technology that will become cost-effective within two years and has the potential to disrupt our production process.'
- **Follow Up**: Investigate the new technology further and consider initiating a pilot project to test its feasibility for integration.
By executing these ChatGPT prompts, you will gain:

- **Insights into Past Performance**
- Clear understanding of past business trends and how they can influence future decisions.
- Recognition of successful products or services and identification of areas needing improvement.
- The knowledge needed to tailor future strategies based on solid historical evidence.

- **Up-to-Date Market Knowledge**
- A current view of the market and how your company's offerings align with it.
- The ability to quickly adjust your business strategies based on real-time market data.

- Insights into consumer expectations and demands that will inform product development and marketing strategies.

- **Preparedness for Future Scenarios**
- Understanding of the potential financial impact of industry-wide changes on your business.
- The ability to plan ahead for cost increases and to make informed decisions about financial risk management.
- The foresight to develop contingency plans that keep your operations running smoothly amidst market fluctuations.

- **Resource Allocation Efficiency**
- Identification of areas where resources can be better utilized for increased revenue and growth.
- An analytical approach to distributing investment into projects based on their potential return.
- Information that will help make decisions that align with strategic growth initiatives, maximizing financial health.

- **Continuous Industry Learning**
- Ongoing updates on technological trends and developments in your sector.
- The know-how to proactively adapt and innovate in response to emerging technologies.
- Strategic insights that enable you to anticipate and capitalize on market shifts, giving you a competitive edge.

These prompts are designed to enhance your strategic planning skills, enrich your business acumen, and ensure that you remain a well-informed decision-maker in a rapidly evolving business world. They provide clarity and depth, ensuring you can confidently navigate the intricacies of your industry.

Spotify's user-centric growth model is a masterclass in business scaling, akin to building a restaurant where the menu evolves daily to fit the customers' tastes. They utilized streams of data on listening habits to tailor playlists and recommendations, much like a chef who crafts dishes based on patrons' favorite ingredients. This personalized experience has resonated deeply with users, transforming casual listeners into loyal subscribers and turning Spotify into a household name.

Similarly, Duolingo's use of gamification breathes life into the often monotonous task of language learning, turning it into an engaging game. It is the equivalent of infusing a fitness routine with the dynamics of a video game—users earn points, level up, and compete, which makes the uphill climb of mastering a new language feel more like an exciting adventure than a rigorous academic pursuit. This strategy has not only captivated millions of learners but also cemented Duolingo's position as a leading language learning platform.

Both Spotify and Duolingo exemplify how understanding and prioritizing user experience can lead to exponential growth. By focusing on what keeps users coming back—whether it's a perfectly curated soundtrack or the thrill of earning a new badge—they've unlocked the secret to scaling their businesses successfully, anchoring their growth strategies to the very human desire for personalization and enjoyment.

Here is the breakdown of the user-focused growth models for Spotify and Duolingo, detailing the data analytics, user engagement, and product development tactics instrumental to their success:

- **Spotify's User-Centric Model**
  - **Data Analytics Techniques**
    - Behavioral analysis: Tracks what users listen to and how they interact with different features.
    - Pattern recognition: Uses algorithms to detect genres or artists that are trending among specific user groups.
    - Personalized recommendations: Creates unique playlists like 'Discover Weekly' based on individual listening habits.
  - **User Engagement Metrics**
    - Stream counts: Tallies the number of times a song is played as a measure of popularity.
    - Skip rates: Evaluates how often users skip a song to gauge satisfaction.
    - Playtime duration: Monitors how long users stay on the platform to determine engagement levels.
  - **Product Development Processes**
    - Iterative design: Continuously refines features based on user feedback.
    - A/B testing: Compares different app versions to select the features that perform best among users.
    - Collaboration features: Develops social elements that allow users to

156

share and discover music together.

- Duolingo's Gamification Strategy
- Data Analytics Techniques
- Learning progress tracking: Monitors how much of a language a user has learned to tailor future lessons.
- Mistake analysis: Identifies common errors to offer personalized corrective exercises.
- Engagement trends: Assesses when and how users are most likely to engage with the app for optimal content delivery.
- User Engagement Metrics
- Streaks: Counts the number of consecutive days users study to encourage consistency.
- Experience points (XP): Tallies points earned for completed lessons and exercises.
- Achievement badges: Rewards milestones and accomplishments to incentivize learning.
- Product Development Processes
- User feedback loop: Incorporates suggestions and responses from the community to refine the learning experience.
- Dynamic leveling: Adapts difficulty based on user performance, keeping the challenge appropriate to skill level.
- Content updates: Regularly refreshes lessons and exercises to keep the material current and engaging.

The meticulous attention to user behavior and satisfaction by both Spotify and Duolingo showcases the power of placing users at the center of the product evolution process. Personalized experiences and a focus on keeping users actively engaged have allowed these companies to remain competitive and grow sustainably. By tapping into detailed data analytics and aligning product development with user needs, they continue to cement their positions as leaders in their respective industries.

As this chapter closes, it's clear that strategic planning and scaling are cornerstones in the architecture of a successful business. They act not just as blueprints, but as the very tools to turn vision into reality. Strategic planning is the map that navigates a company through the competitive landscape, plotting a course that accounts for both opportunities and potential pitfalls. Scaling, on the other hand, is the process of expanding a venture's capabilities without losing its core essence or operational integrity.

Key takeaways underscore the importance of anticipating market trends, understanding customer needs, and investing in the right technology and people. A well-conceived strategy identifies clear objectives and the paths to achieve them, while effective scaling ensures the company grows at a pace that maintains quality and value. This balance is crucial; just as a tree grows both upward and outward, a business must expand its reach while deepening its roots in fundamental principles and practices.

In this journey, leaders are the stewards of growth, the cultivators of culture, and the guardians of the company's mission. Their foresight, decision-making, and adaptability are invaluable as they steer the business through the ever-changing waters of the marketplace. Remember, a business's journey of growth is not a sprint but a marathon—a nuanced and continuous path where strategic planning and scalability are the steady strides that propel it forward.

CONCLUSION

As we conclude our exploration of starting and nurturing a business with ChatGPT, we reflect on the remarkable journey that has unfolded across these pages. At its core, this book has illuminated the transformative potential of integrating artificial intelligence, specifically ChatGPT, into the very fabric of entrepreneurial endeavors.

Key themes have woven through each chapter, such as the unrivaled power of AI in enhancing decision-making, driving innovation, and personalizing customer experiences. We've seen how ChatGPT can serve not only as a tireless assistant but as a wellspring of ideas and an oracle of market trends – a multifaceted tool that reshapes the contours of how businesses operate.

The lessons learned here extend beyond technical know-how. They thrust us into a new paradigm where agility and creativity are paramount, where businesses can not only respond to changes but anticipate and craft them. We've witnessed the former frontiers of business management dissolve, as ChatGPT helps us to map uncharted territories with confidence and precision.

"How To Start A Business With ChatGPT" journey underscores the significance of marrying technology with human insight. We leave this book equipped with the knowledge to harness AI not as a replacement but as a complement to our uniquely human skills – empathy, intuition, ethical discernment – thus forming the ultimate partnership in business success.

As you, the reader, stand at the threshold of your entrepreneurial path, let these final thoughts be the gentle push you need. View ChatGPT not just as a tool but as a collaborator in the art of business. Let the lessons imparted empower you to embark on ventures that are as resilient as they are innovative. With the partnership between human and machine becoming ever more intertwined, the question that now beckons is not whether AI will be integral to the future of business, but how you will redefine that future through your vision and the extraordinary capabilities of AI like ChatGPT.

ABOUT THE AUTHOR

Jon Adams is a Prompt Engineer for Green Mountain Computing specializing and focusing on helping businesses to become more efficient within their own processes and pro-active automation.

Jon@GreenMountainComputing.com

Made in the USA
Las Vegas, NV
15 April 2024

88729644R00089